Clue →↗

CAR CARE

FOR KIDS AND FORMER KIDS

by HARVEY G. LORD

PHOTOGRAPHS by KATHRYN J. LORD

ATHENEUM • 1984 • NEW YORK

LIBRARY OF CONGRESS CATALOGING IN PUBLICATION DATA

Lord, Harvey G.
  Car care for kids—and former kids.

Includes index.
SUMMARY: A basic manual of car maintenance and
repair providing a list of tools needed and
assessing the level of difficulty for each project.
  1. Automobiles—Maintenance and repair—
Juvenile literature.   [1. Automobiles—
Maintenance and repair]
I. Lord, Kathryn J., ill.   II. Title.
TL152.L625   1983   629.28'722   82-13778
ISBN 0-689-30975-9

Text copyright © 1983 by Harvey G. Lord
Photographs copyright © 1983 by Kathryn J. Lord
Published simultaneously in Canada by
McClelland & Stewart, Ltd.
Type set by Linoprint Composition, New York City
Printed and bound by Fairfield Graphics,
Fairfield, Pennsylvania
Designed by Richard Trask
First Printing July 1983
Second Printing May 1984
Third Printing November 1984

CONTENTS

ACKNOWLEDGEMENTS

Like skiing, playing the piano, and brushing your teeth, fixing cars is hard to explain. You need to do it or watch someone else do it in order to completely understand. Still, books help a lot.

Everyone needs help sometimes, and I've had a lot on this book. When you are working on a car and have trouble, the people closest to you can help the most. My wife, Kathy, and my parents, Al and Ethel, have read this manuscript and made many suggestions. I accepted most of them because they made the book better. Kathy also took the photographs. Without her this book would not be worth looking at.

The kids in the pictures were great. My son, Joel, helped the most: working on cars and helping others work on them. Ali Karmel did some heroic work on a valve cover (and other things) that deserves more thanks than I can give. David Ring and Edward and Noelle Gray also worked on different cars for pictures. I hope they all learned something they can use.

Wherever there are cars and kids there are owners and parents. T.C. Karmel, Susan Weldon, and Gail Gray lent time, automobiles, and kids for this project. Linda Duckstein, Bob Lachapelle, and Linda O'Brien allowed me to photograph their car's engines. Thanks to everyone and double thanks.

Some auto parts, tools, and tires photographed here were borrowed. Armand Fontaine of the Ideal Tire Company (Willimantic, Connecticut) helped whenever I asked by lending me tires and tire stands as well as explanations. Bob Napack of Stan's Auto Parts (Willimantic, Connecticut) lent hundreds of dollars worth of tools for pictures. Reno Nadeau of Gem Chevrolet (Mansfield, Connecticut) spent time showing me cars and talking about their engines when he knew I wasn't going to buy anything. Al Gobin lent me tools and, more important, expert advice. I sincerely thank all of them. They're first-rate people.

Finally, there are Atheneum Publishers and Marcia Marshall, the publisher and editor of this book. Without them, you couldn't read this.

Have fun working on your car, learn things, and don't be afraid or embarrassed to ask for help. If I didn't explain something clearly enough for you, there is probably someone near you who can do a better job. Ask.

Harvey G. Lord

1. BASICS

This book explains how you can repair and maintain an automobile.* The early chapters are the easiest and the later ones are harder. But, if you can read this, you are old enough to do the work. I know you don't know anything about cars, but you *are* old enough. When our son, Joel, was born, ten years ago, I knew as much about cars as you do now. I also didn't have enough money to keep paying mechanics for changing oil and lubricating—whatever that was. I started to learn. Surprise, it's simple! Even bigger surprise, Joel started to learn, too.

Today, he can do almost everything in this book and then some. If he and his friends can do it, so can you.

The trick to learning how to fix cars is

*If you are over twenty-one and know nothing about cars (besides the fact that they eat money), this is for you, too.

doing only a little at a time. Each single part is simple. The whole machine is complicated. If you only look at the air filter, you can understand and replace it. If you look at the whole engine, it's too complex to know where to begin.

Each chapter looks at one, or very few, parts. You see what they do and why they might wear out or need replacing. After that, you do the work. What parts and tools to buy, where to get them, and their prices are covered. Tools' uses are illustrated. Some tools, like wheel chocks when jacking the car (see Chapters 14 and 15), are lying on the ground for the taking. Free is my favorite price.

Every chapter talks about safety. Car repair is fun unless you get hurt. The most important thing you own is *you*. Even a car standing still is dangerous if you can't control it. Cars roll. Cars have electrical systems. If you know how to stop the roll or keep from getting shocked, no problem. If not, look out. Except for checking some cars' automatic transmission fluid (Chapter 6), all repairs in this book require that the engine be off. The car always stands still. The parking brake is always on. If you don't know how to put on the parking brake, ask the car's owner. Always park the car on a level place, *off* the street. Never try to fix a car on the road. Follow the safety rules and avoid accidents in the first place.

All auto fluids except water and air are poisonous. Most will burn. Keep them away from little children and flames.

Adults know that cars are dangerous. They may wonder if you can do auto repairs. You must show them that you're careful and able. Before asking for permission to do a job, read the chapter carefully. Know exactly what you're going to do and how to do it. Then, when asking for permission, invite the car's owner to watch. Ask him or her to read the chapter, too. When the owner sees that you know what you're doing, permission will be easier to get for the next job. After a while, you'll be able to work on your own.

When asking for permission to do car work, ask for parts and tools money, too. Why should the owner give you money for buying things? The answer is, to save money. When a professional mechanic works on a car, the bill is for the cost of three things: (1) tools, (2) parts, and (3) time. The time includes time to buy the tools, the parts, and do the work. The mechanic bought the tools years ago, but you still pay for them with each repair bill. Why not save all that money? Use it to pay for tools yourself. On the second job, the tools are all paid for and you still save money. After a while, the owner can save from half to three-quarters (or more) of the price of auto repair work.

There is another reason for doing this work yourself. When you own a car, you will know how to do a lot of things most car owners can't do. Then, it will be your money you save. Also, if you play your cards right and do a good job, you might get some pay for the work right now. After all, if you do the work properly, you should get paid.

Most chapters in this book are complete by themselves. You don't have to read one chapter in order to understand another. Therefore, you can read about you car's problems in any order. Sometimes an explanation is repeated in several chapters. Then, you can skip it

because it's the same as an earlier chapter. Odometer use (figuring how far the car has gone since the last oil or filter change) works that way. Other times, you must reread an earlier chapter's explanation. Those situations are marked when you come to them.

At the beginning of each chapter, there is a list of information about the chapter's work: (1) difficulty, (2) parts needed, (3) tools needed, and (4) help needed. Early chapters explain simple jobs. They use few tools and parts. The car's owner may be invited to watch, but need not help. If you've never done any auto work, these are perfect projects to start on. If early chapters seem too easy, try later ones. They're harder and may be more interesting. Still, don't skip over the first chapters because they're easy. Changing the oil, air filter, and oil filter, and checking fluid levels are important. They need doing. Besides, the work in later chapters sometimes requires help. If you've never worked on cars before, start at the beginning.

"The beginning" is a car's owner's manual. It's usually in the glove compartment. If you can't find it, ask the car's owner for it. Then, *read it*. If the manual is lost, a substitute is necessary. An auto repair handbook for your specific car is published by the Clymer's Publication Company and the Chilton Book Company. It costs about eight to twelve dollars in an auto parts store and includes a lot more information than a regular owner's manual. Read Chapter 18 for more about Clymer's, Chilton's, and other manuals.

Unlike Clymer's and Chilton's handbooks, this book explains every step for each job. Still, every car is different. The pictures here only show certain cars. Yours may not look the same. If, when you begin to work on a car, you can't find a part, ask a local gasoline station mechanic to point it out for you. Remember, though, mechanics are not teachers. They're busy and may not want to help. If they do, they're doing you a favor. Only ask one question at a time and make it short. For example, if you can't find the oil drain plug, only ask about that. Never ask a mechanic to explain the whole job. If one person will not help, go to another station. Be polite and someone will answer your question.

As you learn about cars, you'll want to do more. Of course, there's much more that can be done. No book can tell everything about any subject. The last chapter here suggests where to look for more.

If you only do the jobs in this book, you'll still do more than most car owners. You'll also save the car owner's money. Then, when you buy your own car, you can save your own money by doing the work yourself. Finally, and most important, whatever car you work on now, really *is* your car. Maybe you don't own it, but you take care of it. Follow the directions carefully and you can have more than money. You can have pride in doing first-rate work, too.

Now, proud person, wash your hands. They are filthy. Even though cars are dirty and oily, you must be able to clean your hands after working on them. The most common way to do that is to wash them with soap and water. When they get very dirty, strong hand soap is used. Boraxo, Lava, or Fels Naptha are sold in supermarkets for scrubbing grimy hands. Auto parts and department stores also sell soft hand soap for *very* dirty hands. If necessary, use both the strong hand soap and the soft soap together. That takes off almost any dirt.

If you must hold your hands in kerosene or lacquer thinner (see Chapter 17), wear rubber gloves. They are easy to wash and no one cares if they're not completely clean. Inside rubber gloves, hands stay spotless. Of course, for most work, rubber gloves are bulky and uncomfortable.

Finally, some mechanics use a cream called Pro-Tek. It costs about three dollars for one tube and is rubbed on your hands *before* starting work. It keeps oil, grease, and dirt from sticking to skin. When you finish the job, washing with plain soap and water removes the mess and the Pro-Tek together. No hard scrubbing is needed. While it doesn't protect as well as rubber gloves, it does work. As long as no harsh liquids (kerosene or lacquer thinner, for example) touch your hands, Pro-Tek works well.

Now for the car work. Roll up your sleeves. Get your soap, rubber gloves, or Pro-Tek ready. Go to it.

2. AIR FILTERS

Difficulty: Easy
Parts: New air filter
Tools: A pliers
Hand soap and/or Pro-Tek (see Ch. 1)
Help needed: None

Most of the things under the hood are made of steel, but some important parts of cars are made of paper. Gasoline, oil, and even the air a car needs must be cleaned before going into the engine. That's done with paper filters, something like coffee filters.

Few people realize that cars need air. Small amounts of gasoline are carefully burned inside auto engines, but unless the gasoline is mixed with air first, it won't burn. In fact, nothing will burn without a gas in air called oxygen.

Fortunately for all of us who do not think about air, auto designers do think of it. In order to burn gasoline without waste, it must be carefully mixed with air. This is done in the carburetor. Since only a few drops of gasoline burn at one time, the carburetor must have very tiny holes (called "jets") to squirt gasoline through. Some of these jets are so small that a pin won't fit through them.

All autos' power comes from burning gasoline. In most cars, gasoline (squares) and air (circles, the oxygen is the gray circles) mix in the carburetor. The engine then converts the tiny explosions caused by burning the gas into forward movement.

Inside an Auto Engine

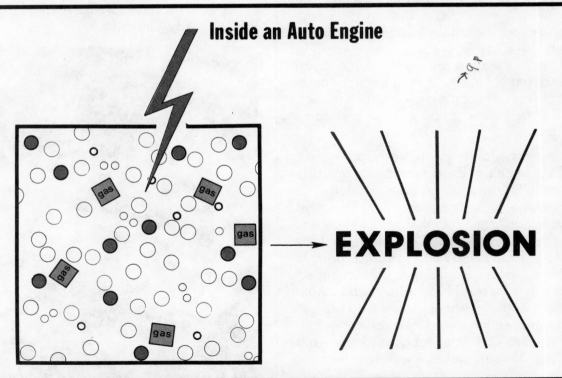

EXPLOSION

6

Since air is everywhere, it's free and easy to get. It's also often very dirty. Even a tiny piece of dirt can clog the carburetor jets. Worse, if some dirt gets through the carburetor it will scratch and wear the engine's insides. That shortens the engine's life, makes it run poorly, and wastes expensive gasoline.

To make sure that the air going in is clean, auto designers put an air filter on top of the carburetor. As air is sucked into the carburetor, it goes through the filter,

A car's owner's manual always tells when the air filter should be changed. In some cars, it needs to be replaced every twelve thousand (12,000) miles. Others can wait until the car has gone about twenty-four thousand (24,000) miles. If the car rides in dirty air (like on dirt roads), the air filter must be changed much more often than the owner's manual says.

To see how many miles the car has traveled, look at the dashboard. In the middle of the speedometer is a line of

Air moves through the air intake and into the air filter housing as the arrows show. It's sucked through the air filter, which removes dirt and dust. Then, it goes into the carburetor to be mixed with gasoline.

Subtract the proper number (for this job) on the driver's door sticker (left) from the number on the odometer (right). Ignore the odometer's right-hand digit.

which catches bits of dirt or dust. Clean air comes out the other side, ready for mixing with the gasoline. Then, the mixture is sucked into the engine and burned.

Of course, after a while the paper filter gets dirty. A dirty filter makes it hard for the engine to get enough air. This wastes gasoline, makes the engine run poorly, and creates pollution. Because air filters need changing every now and then, auto designers make reaching and replacing them easy.

        43,155 (odometer reading)
      −31,200 (air filter number on driver's door)
        11,955 (remainder)

The remainder is the number of miles the car has been driven since the last air filter change. The owner's manual for this car says air filters should be changed every twelve thousand (12,000), give or take a few, miles. Since 11,955 is close to 12,000, it is time to do the job.

numbers that change as the car moves. This is the odometer. It tells how many miles the car has gone. Write down the number that appears there, except for the last digit on the right. On the edge of the driver's door, there's usually a sticker that tells the odometer reading when the car was last serviced and what was done. Find out from that sticker or ask the car's owner the odometer reading when the air filter was last changed. Subtract that number from the present odometer reading. The remainder is the number of miles the car has gone since changing air filters.

If your owner's manual and odometer say that it is time to change the filter (and the car's owner agrees), you can do it yourself. By changing your own filter, you save money because no one needs to get paid to change the filter for you. You also get to see inside part of the carburetor.

Before taking anything apart, go to an auto parts store and buy an air filter to fit your *make, model,* and *year* of car. Sometimes, you need to know whether the engine has four, six, or eight cylinders and the engine displacement (a measure of the exact engine size). This information is always in the owner's manual. Take the manual to the store if you're not sure. You don't need to know the brand name of an air filter or any special part number.

Air filters cost about four or five dollars. Sometimes, department or auto parts stores put them on sale for half the usual price. Don't worry that the filters on sale aren't as good as more expensive ones. All automobile air filters that fit your car work perfectly well.

Before changing the air filter, be sure your car is turned off and sitting still on level ground. The parking brake must be on. Wear old clothes. If you want to use it, now is the time to put on Pro-Tek, the

protective hand cream.

Under the hood on top of the engine there is a round steel box with a horn sticking out of one side. That's the air filter housing and the horn-shaped thing is the air

Ed is unscrewing the wing nut from the air filter housing. Screwing *off* is done counterclockwise (arrow). Screwing *on* is done clockwise. Some air filter housings have washers under the wing nut. Replace them under the nut when you finish the job.

Now, Ed must loosen the clips on the sides of the housing (arrow). The arrows on the air intake and housing lid must point to each other when he replaces the lid.

intake. The air filter fits inside the housing and is not held down by anything except the lid.

On top of most air filter housings is a wing nut that holds the lid on. Sometimes the wing nut is loose enough to twist with your fingers. If yours is, no tools are needed to change your own air filter. If the wing nut is screwed on hard, a pliers will loosen it. Twist the wing nut loose (counterclockwise), then turn it off with your fingers. If there are any washers under the

wing nut, carefully put them aside. Do *not* lose them. A few cars have no wing nuts, only little clips on the sides of the air filter housing. You need no tools to remove them. Open any clips or fasteners holding on the lid with your hands. Then remove the lid and put it with the wing nut and washers.

Pick up the old air filter. Put your new air filter into the housing where the old one was. Usually, either side of it can go up. Make sure it's in the center of the housing. Right in the middle of the filter is a hole that fits over the top part of the carburetor. Do not drop anything, even the smallest bit of dirt, in there.

All that is left of the job is putting the lid back. Sometimes the housing is not exactly round and the lid fits on only one way. When that happens, the lid usually has an arrow pointing to another arrow on the air intake. Line up the two arrows and the lid will fit perfectly. Replace the washers and wing nut and tighten the fasteners on the sides of the lid. Tighten the wing nut as firmly as you can with your fingers. Do *no* use the pliers.

You've just replaced an air filter as v as any professional mechanic. Save odometer reading in the glove com ment. You'll need it to know wh change the filter again.

Next time you think abou remember that it's more than j thing to write on. You can take filter apart to see the dirty pa protected your car's engine several thousand miles. Oth use something like toilet pa a car's oil, but that's anothe come to that in Chapter 5

On another car, Ed replaces the air filter. In the center of the housing, the top of the carburetor lets in air. No dirt is allowed there. On this car, there is no wing nut, just side clips. Every car is different.

3. MOTOR OIL

Difficulty: Easy
Parts: Motor oil
Tools: Rags
Can opener
Hand soap and/or Pro-Tek (see Ch. 1)
Help needed: None

Cars grind themselves to bits. Even when the engine is working properly, the parts rubbing together are turning into bits of steel powder. This is normal, but definitely not good. It wears out the engine. Therefore, automobile designers do everything they can to slow down this wear. One of the tricks they use is covering everything inside the engine with messy, slippery oil.

Imagine all the gears, rods, pistons, and wheels in an engine moving at thousands of turns every minute. When a piston pushes a rod which turns a wheel, pieces of steel touch others. When metal touches other metal, constant produces friction.

hands together and rub them as you can. You feel heat. ed by the friction of rubbing enough, you might

same thing, mostly Of course, steel is ke a lot more n. Still, cars on't know to hurt. akens eak as the

Pouring oil over all the rubbing parts in an engine makes them slippery. This is called lubrication. It doesn't completely stop the rubbing. It doesn't completely prevent bits of metal from turning into dust, but it does slow down the wearing out and makes the engine run better.

When oil is pumped through the engine, it takes some of the heat away from sliding surfaces. Oil that touches rubbing steel gets hot. When it's pumped away, it takes heat with it.

Finally, the motor oil flowing through the engine carries bits of steel dust away from moving engine parts. This protects them from the extra grinding of steel dust trapped between rubbing surfaces. Oil, which we think is dirty, actually helps clean the engine.

Oil can only clean, cool, and lubricate an engine if there's enough of it around. The dipstick is for checking motor oil. It's a steel rod (usually with a curly top) often sticking up at an angle from the engine. The end of the dipstick sits in a pool of oil at the engine's bottom. When this pool is deep enough, there's enough oil for proper lubrication.

It's a good idea to check the oil at least once a week. Properly running engines use oil very slowly. But a car might spring a leak and lose its oil without anyone knowing it if someone does not check. Besides, the only tool needed is a rag.

Make sure the car's owner agrees that you may check the oil and that the car is parked with the engine *off* on a level surface. If the car is on a hill, the oil level reading may be wrong. The parking brake must be on and the car should sit still for at least ten minutes before you check the oil.

Arrows point to motor oil dipsticks. Dipsticks always look pretty much the same, but are located in different places in different engines. Don't confuse the motor oil dipstick with the automatic transmission dipstick (Chapter 6). If you aren't sure, ask a mechanic.

Wear old clothes because oil sometimes drips. If you want to use Pro-Tek, put it on now.

Grab the end of the dipstick and pull it out of its tube. It should come right out. If it doesn't, you may be grabbing something else. Do *not* pull hard. If you can't find the dipstick, ask a gasoline station attendant to point at it the next time you go to a gas station.

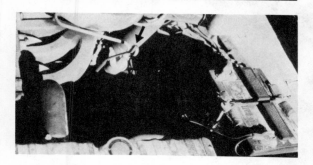

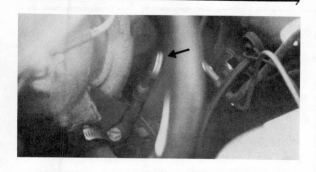

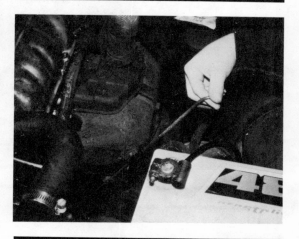

Joel pulls the dipstick out of its tube after the car is shut off.

At the end of the dipstick are marks covered with oil. Wipe off the stick completely with a rag and put it all the way back into its tube. Then, pull it out again to see where the line of oil hits those marks. One mark will say "F" for full. Another usually says "L" for low. If there's not enough, add oil right away. Running a car with too little oil is one of the quickest ways to wreck the engine. Whether the oil level is low or not, replace the dipstick in its tube as soon as you've checked it. Never put the dipstick down on anything that might be dirty.

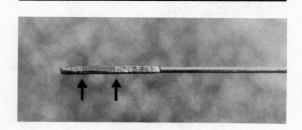

Joel cleans the dipstick before putting it back into its tube to check the oil level. Arrows indicate the F (full) and L (low) marks on the dipstick.

In order to add oil, you must buy some. Motor oil is sold in auto parts, department, and some grocery stores and supermarkets. It costs about one dollar for one quart and is sometimes on sale. Some people say that one oil company makes

better oil than the others, but all brands work well. No matter what kind or brand of motor oil you buy, it must be oil made for automobiles. Oil for chainsaws, snowmobiles, or outboard motor boats may not be right for cars. To be sure that the oil is for cars, look for the following special sentences printed on the oil can. If the can or bottle of oil says that it "meets" or "exceeds car manufacturers' warranty requirements" or "specifications," that oil is made for cars. A few oil companies abbreviate this sentence. Some only say "for service MS." Others say "for API service SD or SE." The oil can must say at least one of the above or it is probably not made for cars.

Be sure to buy motor oil that's the proper thickness for your car and the time of year. The thickness or "weight" of oil tells you how fast the oil will flow. The numbers on oil cans reveal its thickness. In summer, when it's warm, thicker oil is needed than in cold, winter weather. For winter, buy 10W-30 oil. For summer, 10W-40 is usually good. Your car's owner's manual says which kind is best for your car.

Adding motor oil is sometimes messy, so again, wear old clothes. Be sure the car is standing still on level ground. The parking brake must be on and the engine off. If you like, now's the time to put on Pro-Tek.

On or near the top center of most engines is a metal cap about three inches across. This is the oil filler cap. Do *not* confuse it with some other cap. A car may have three or four caps under the hood. Some cars have special oil filler pipes. If necessary, ask a mechanic to point yours out. Grab the cap with your hands and twist it off. If it's slippery, you may have to clean it with a rag or grab it with a rag in your hand. It should come off without tools. You may need help from an adult, but oil caps never rust on because oil prevents rust. Never pour oil into the wrong opening. Such a mistake could be very expensive.

Open the oil can with an old-fashioned can opener, the kind that makes a V-shaped hole in the top of the can. (Everyone used to have these before pop-tops were invented.) Be sure to put two holes in the can, across the top from each other. This allows oil to pour smoothly. Then, carefully pour the oil through the oil filler hole. If you can't reach the filler hole, stand on a stool. Don't spill oil. If the dipstick says your engine is one quart low, add one quart of the proper oil. Be very careful and don't get *any* dirt in the oil. Then, replace the oil filler cap all the way.

After letting the oil drain for one or two minutes into the bottom of the engine, take the dipstick out again to see if the oil level reaches the "Full" mark. If not, add more. Do *not* overfill. Too much oil in the engine is a waste. It can get all over the inside of the engine compartment, making a mess. It may also damage engine parts. Remember to put the *clean* dipstick back into its tube immediately after checking the oil level.

After a while, of course, adding oil won't be enough. As time goes by, the engine's oil gets dirty and it won't do its job properly. When that happens, all the engine oil must be changed. Fortunately, that's pretty easy, too. The next chapter tells you how.

Ali opens a can of motor oil with a can opener. She puts holes on both sides of the top so oil can flow smoothly.

Joel pours oil into the proper filler hole. He doesn't need a special spout on the oil can. A little care and nothing is spilled.

4. CHANGING OIL

Difficulty: Easy
Parts: Motor oil
Tools: Wrench (adjustable, socket, open end, box, or combination)
Can opener
Shallow tub (that fits under the engine)
Empty plastic milk bottles
Funnel
Rags
Cat litter
Hand soap and/or Pro-Tek (see Ch. 1)
Help needed: None

Motor oil is like bath water. Water cools you off in hot weather and floats dirt from your body. If the water gets too dirty though, it leaves scum on you as you leave the tub. Oil does the same thing. It cleans and cools the engine as long as it's not too dirty. However, after long use, the oil may actually leave more dirt on engine parts than it cleans. Used oil may also have chemicals in it that can hurt an engine.

Usually bath water is only used once. Then, it drains away. Oil, on the other hand, gets used over and over. It sits at the bottom of the engine in the oil pan when the engine is off. When the engine is turned on, the oil flows through it only to drain back into the oil pan to be pumped around again. This recycling saves oil. Unfortunately, like reusing bath water, it means the oil eventually becomes very dirty and can no longer lubricate properly.

After driving some cars only 1,500 miles, the oil must be changed completely. Other cars go 3,000 and some 6,000 miles before they need an oil change. Still others can go 12,000 miles. The owner's manual says how long to use oil before changing it.

Check the odometer in the center of the speedometer on the dashboard to find out how many miles the car has gone since the last oil change. Write down the present odometer reading. From it, subtract the number from the driver's door sticker that says when the oil was last changed. The remainder is the number of miles driven since the last oil change. If that number is the same as the number in the owner's manual, it's time to change the oil.

Be sure you have enough oil to fill the engine before draining any. Again, the owner's manual says how much oil the car needs. Buy enough 10W-30 or 10W-40 motor oil (reread Chapter 3 about oil) to fill up the engine after draining the old oil and replacing the drain plug.

Also, before draining any oil, be sure you have the proper tools ready. You need a rag or two, an old, shallow tub to catch the oil, an old milk jug or two to hold the used oil, a funnel with which to pour the old oil into the bottle or jug, a wrench to open the oil drain plug, and some cat litter to help clean up spilled oil. The wrench can be an adjustable one or a socket wrench or open-end or box wrench of the proper size. A combination wrench—with an open end at one end and a box end at the other—works fine.

Consider their uses before choosing your tools. The tub for catching oil can be an old plastic dishwashing tub or shallow clothes washing tub. It must fit under the car and not be needed elsewhere. Once it holds motor oil, it's too dirty for most other things. Empty plastic milk bottles with caps are good for storing old oil. The funnel for pouring must be carefully cleaned before and after each use. If you don't clean it, don't use it for other things. Whichever wrench you use, it must be the longest one you can find because the oil drain plug is actually a big bolt. It's usually very tight.

Ali smears Pro-Tek on her hands. It makes washing much easier.

Because a little oil is bound to spill, be sure that the car is parked in a garage or parking lot where a little oil doesn't matter. *Never* change oil with the car parked on the street. Crawling under a car on the street is very dangerous. Someone might run over your legs while you are underneath. The car must be on a level surface with the parking brake on. The engine must be off. This is a messy job: wear old clothes. If you plan to use Pro-Tek to keep oil and dirt from sticking to your hands, put it on now. Have hand soap ready.

The best time to change oil is right after driving somewhere for at least ten minutes. Driving heats oil, making it flow faster. Cold oil flows very slowly, taking a long

Ali turns the oil drain plug with an adjustable wrench. She tried to turn it with the wrench before, but couldn't. Then, she put a piece of long pipe over the handle. Now she can loosen the plug easily. Adjust the wrench so it fits the plug snugly.

time to drain. Some never drains out at all. Hot oil drains completely.

The drain plug is underneath the car, toward the front, on the bottom of the oil pan. If you can't find it, ask a gas station mechanic to point at it. Be sure the tub to catch oil is under the oil pan when you open the plug. Oil will gush out. Whatever kind of wrench you use, it must be the right size. That is, the wrench must fit the head of the drain plug exactly. If you use an adjustable wrench, tighten it around the bolt head so it doesn't wobble. Loosen the plug. If you can't turn it, try jerking the wrench handle. Be sure you're turning in the proper direction. All standard screws and bolts loosen counterclockwise and tighten clockwise. Look at a round clock face to remember which way it turns. If jerking the wrench doesn't work, find a long piece of pipe that fits over the wrench handle. With the pipe on the handle, place the wrench on the bolt head again. Pull the end of the pipe. That should loosen the plug. Turn the plug out with your fingers, but be careful. The oil is hot and it can burn. Be ready to pull your hands away quickly. If you drop the drain plug into the tub, don't worry. You can find it later when the oil is cool.

After about ten minutes the tub should be filled with dirty oil. The engine is empty. If it's time to change the oil filter (read Chapter 5), do it now. Carefully clean the oil drain plug and make sure that any washers that were on the threads are still there. Those washers seal the drain plug so that oil can't leak. Everything must be very clean before putting it back. After all the oil drains, screw the drain plug and washers back. Tighten them with the wrench. The drain plug should be pretty tight, but not as tight as you can turn. You might ruin the plug's threads by tightening too much.

Finally, the oil filler cap under the car's hood is removed for refilling the engine with oil. Follow the directions in Chapter 4. Don't overfill the engine! After putting in new oil and replacing the oil filler cap,

most people think they're finished with the job. Nope. Now comes the important part.

You have a tub full of old, dirty motor oil. Some people pour it on the ground (messy pollution) or down the sewer (illegal pollution). Please don't do either. Pour your oil into one or more plastic milk bottles or jugs using the funnel, and try not to spill any. Cap the jug.

Have the car's owner move the car. Then spread cat litter on any oily spots. It soaks up the oil and you can sweep it away later into the garbage. Be careful not to track oil into the house because it makes troublesome stains. Wash your hands to remove the dirt and Pro-Tek (if you used it). If necessary, use Boraxo, Lava, Fels Naptha, or some other strong soap to clean your hands.

In my town, the health department handles the dirty motor oil problem. They have a tank at the town dump for old oil. If you know where waste oil is collected in your town, take it there. If you don't, phone your town hall and ask them to whom you should talk about proper disposal of used motor oil.

Sometimes, you can take the used oil to a local gasoline station. Most stations have huge underground tanks for storing used motor oil. When they're full, a tank truck pumps them out. The old oil can be cleaned and reprocessed; there are special uses for it.

In any case, please don't dump the old oil on the ground. It kills plants and, if you're near a water source, it can poison fish, animals, and even people. Now that you've helped your car run better, spend some time getting rid of the old oil properly to help the world run better.

Ali pours old oil into a milk bottle and Joel puts cat litter on an oil spill in the parking lot. Later, the cat litter is swept into the trash.

Joel pours old motor oil into a tank for recycling waste oil at the town dump. Please get rid of old oil properly. Don't pollute.

WASTE OILS

5. OIL FILTERS

Difficulty: Easy to moderate
Parts: New oil filter
Tools: Oil filter wrench
Help needed: None

NOTE: Oil filter changing is done during an oil change.

Just as dirty motor oil is cleaned and recycled after draining, a car's oil is recycled all the time. It drains into the oil pan and gets pumped back up into the engine to do its work again. Since it gets dirty while being reused, auto designers build oil cleaning systems into cars. They don't work forever, so oil must be changed anyway, but they work for a while. This cleaning system uses an oil filter.

Just like the air filter, the oil filter is made of paper, something like a roll of toilet paper. After running through the engine, the oil is forced through many paper layers, which hold the tiny bits of steel dust. The oil coming out the other side is much cleaner than the oil that went in.

Of course, even a very good oil filter gets clogged with dirt after a while and must be changed. Again, the owner's manual tells when to change oil filters. Usually, they need changing every other time the oil is changed. Since oil filters are only changed when there is no oil in the engine, filter replacement is really part of the oil change job. Before putting the drain plug back and putting in new oil, you need to replace the oil filter *if* the odometer and owner's manual say to. Check the odometer and sticker on the edge of the driver's door. Subtract the sticker number from the present odometer reading. If the re-

mainder is about the same as the figure in the owner's manual, change the oil filter. If you don't know when it was changed last, do it now.

Before draining any oil, be sure you have a new oil filter and oil filter wrench. Oil filters are sold in auto parts, department, and some drug stores. New ones cost about three to five dollars, but are sometimes on sale for half that. The cheapest one is the best because they all do the job. Ask for an oil filter to fit your *make, model,* and *year* of car. Sometimes the engine size is needed, too. That's listed in the owner's manual, which you can take with you to the store. For most oil filters, the back of the box lists which cars the filter fits. Check the box to see if your car is listed.

An oil filter wrench isn't always necessary, but you should have one just in case the old filter is stuck on. An oil filter wrench costs from $1.50 to $5.00 and makes the whole job much easier. It looks like a big ring with a handle sticking out the side. Buy one on which the ring is just a little bigger than your oil filter. Oil filter wrenches are usually sold near the new filters. Expensive ones may not be better than cheaper ones.

Now go back to Chapter 4 and drain out the motor oil. While it drains, find the oil filter on the engine. It usually sticks out the side and is mounted pointing sideways or at an angle. Sometimes, it's in a difficult place to reach, but some car makers think about the person servicing the car. They design their machines so that reaching the oil filter is easy. If you ever buy a new car, look to see where the oil filter is. Think about how hard it is to

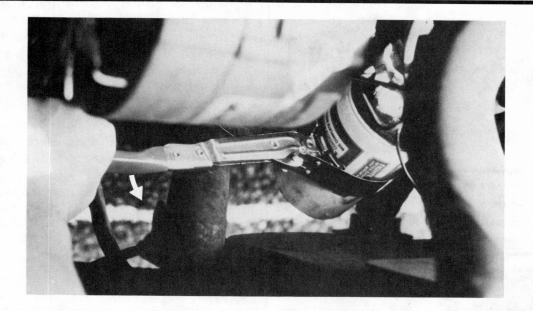

David removes the old oil filter with a filter wrench. Remove filters by turning as the arrow indicates. Place an old tub under the filter to catch oil drips.

replace. If you can't find the oil filter on your car, ask a service station mechanic to point to it.

When all the oil is drained from the engine, position the old tub under the oil filter. Try to turn the old filter off with your hands. It's usually stuck, but sometimes it can be twisted off. If you can get it off by hand, the filter wrench is not necessary. If the wrench is needed, place the ring around the old filter with the handle pointing left. As you press the handle toward the filter and turn counterclockwise, the ring tightens around the filter and the wrench helps loosen it. When the filter is loose, remove the wrench and turn the filter by hand.

Don't drop the filter after it comes off. It's filled with oil even after all the rest of the oil drains from the engine. Try not to spill any, but some almost always drips. The drips should be caught in the old oil tub. If it misses the tub, clean it up after the car is out of the way. Hold the old filter with its hole up. Carefully pour the old oil out by tipping the filter down toward the tub. When the filter is empty, carefully throw it away. Don't drip oil on the ground or you. Never reuse old oil filters.

Before screwing the new filter in place, carefully clean the circle where the new filter will press against the car. Use a clean rag and be sure that there's no dirt or grit on that circle. The smallest piece of dirt can make the new oil you're pouring in leak. When replacing filters, the watchword is CLEAN. Now look at the new oil filter. It has a rubber ring and hole in the bottom. Before installing it, carefully wipe your hands clean with a rag and dip one

19

Joel cleans the place where the rubber on the new filter will touch the car. This is called the "seat." Dirt on the seat may cause oil leaks.

Ali oils the rubber ring on the new filter. This makes it seal on the clean seat. A new filter should be easy to screw on. If it isn't, you're screwing it on crooked. Don't force it. Unscrew, if necessary, and try again.

finger into some clean oil. Place a tiny amount of oil on the rubber ring. Lightly cover *all* the rubber with *clean* oil. This prepares the rubber to stop leaks.

With everything clean and the rubber oiled, carefully screw the new filter into place where the old one was removed. Do *not* use the filter wrench. When the filter begins to get hard to turn with your hands, turn it about one-quarter to one-half turn more. Stop. It doesn't need to be tight, just snug enough to stop leaks. As the engine heats up, the rubber expands and makes the new filter as tight as the old one was.

Now replace the oil drain plug and pour in clean oil as explained in Chapter 4. Be sure to keep the old oil in your oil jug for recycling and clean up the floor with cat litter.

Ask the car's owner to start the car with the hood open. Look at the oil filter to make sure it's not leaking around the rubber seal. If it is, tighten it more. Check the drain plug for leaks, too. Tighten it, if necessary. Turn off the engine before tightening anything. If no tightening is needed, you're done.

If there is oil on your clothes, shoes, or you, clean it with rags as well as possible before going back into the house. *Never* walk around a house with oil on shoes or clothes. Motor oil stains carpets and furniture. Wash with strong soap like Boraxo, Lava, or Fels Naptha. If necessary, wash your shoes, too.

Changing the oil and oil filter and keeping the oil level at full are the most important things you can do to make your car last as long as possible. It would cost you from two to three times the materials' cost to pay a mechanic to do the job. Now you know how easy it really is. The few tools necessary pay for themselves on the first oil and filter change. It would have cost as much as all those tools just to pay someone else to do the work. Next time, you have the tools to use. Besides, if you prove you can do it, the car's owner might just pay you to change the oil next time. How about that for a way to make money?

By the way, remember to write down the present odometer reading and put it in the glove compartment or write it on the door label so that you know when to do the job again.

6. MORE FLUIDS

Difficulty: Easy
Parts: Transmission fluid (as needed)
Brake fluid (as needed)
Power steering fluid (as needed)
Tools: Rags
Masking tape
Marker pen
Hand soap and/or Pro-Tek (see Ch. 1)
Cat litter
Help needed: One adult (maybe)

For all the solid steel, rubber, plastic, and paper in cars, materials that flow, called fluids, really make them go. Of course gasoline and air are fluids. Oil is also a fluid, but there are fluids outside the engine, too. The transmission, brakes, power steering, and some clutches also need special fluids to make them work.

In general, fluids do five different things in cars. Some actually do more than one of these things. (1) Some important fluids burn. Gasoline and air, for example, burn to give the car power. (2) Other fluids make solid parts slippery. This is called lubrication. Motor oil (see Chapters 3-5) lubricates many engine parts. (3) Another fluid (a coolant) cools hot objects in the car's engine and elsewhere. Motor oil and radiator fluid (see Chapter 7) do this. (4) There are also fluids that clean engine parts as the car runs. Motor oil does this, too. (5) Finally, some fluids push against other parts and move them. This is called actuation. Brake fluid is a fluid actuator.

BRAKES

Brake fluid transmits force. It actuates. The brake pedal pushes fluid through tubes called brake lines. At the end of the tubes, the fluid pushes against the wheels' brakes to stop the car. Many years ago, all cars had mechanical brakes. Pressing the brake pedal stopped the car. Today, cars often have power brakes. With them, the brake pedal is a switch to use the car engine's power to assist or help the driver push the fluid. A little push on the power brake pedal makes a big push on the brakes. If the engine is off, there's no power to help. Without that power, the brakes still work, but it takes lots of strength in the driver's leg to stop the car.

As long as the brakes are in good condition, with enough fluid, the car stops when the driver presses the brake pedal. Unfortunately, the brake lines are long, with many connections. Any of them could leak. If they do, there may not be enough fluid to make the brakes work. Or, if the fluid wasn't put in properly when the brakes were serviced, there may seem to be enough brake fluid, but the lines may be partly filled with air. Then, pressing the brake pedal just squashes the air. (Brake fluid does not squash.) So, again, the brakes can't work. Keeping the right amount of break fluid in the lines and making sure there is no air in the lines helps prevent accidents.

You can check fluid levels and, if necessary, add more. Since the amount of brake fluid could save your life, this is well worth the trouble.

There are from one to four or five cups or small tanks under the hood. They are fluid reservoirs. If there's only one, it holds brake fluid. If there are several, go to a gas station and ask the mechanic what each is

The brake reservoirs are usually on the driver's side of the car. They look like little cups made of steel or plastic (arrow).

for. If you can't find any reservoirs, ask where they are. When you find out what fluid is in each reservoir, put a piece of masking tape on the top of each. With the marking pen, write on the tape the name of the fluid in the reservoir. Warning: the wrong fluid in a reservoir can cause serious damage.

Now have the car's owner drive it to a level place away from the road and turn the car off. If the car isn't parked on a level place, the reading may not be right. Set the parking brake. Since you may get dirty doing this, wear old clothes.

Some reservoirs are made of transparent plastic. If your brake fluid reservoirs are, look through their sides to make sure they're full. There's a line near the top of each reservoir that shows how full it should be. If you cannot see through the sides of the reservoirs, unsnap or unscrew the caps. Keep those caps clean. Look inside. If the fluid level is low, but still above the bottom of the reservoir, add more.

If the fluid is completely gone, there's probably air in the brake lines. Replace the reservoir caps immediately. With the

engine *off,* step on the brake pedal. If it feels like you pushed down easily, then suddenly hit a very hard spot, good. That is how brakes should feel. If there's a soft or spongy feeling before you cannot push anymore, bad. That's a sign of air in the brake lines.

If there's air in the lines or if the brake fluid has fallen below the bottom of the reservoir, don't let anyone drive the car! Call a tow truck and take the car to a service station. Cars without working brakes are death traps.

If you just need to add fluid, buy the proper kind at an auto parts or department store. Always buy the cheapest fluid that's graded for your car. More expensive fluids don't necessarily do a better job.

Brake fluid is graded by the Federal Department of Transportation (DOT) and most cars use DOT 3. Some must use DOT 4 brake fluid. The owner's manual says which. *Never* use the cheaper DOT 3 brake fluid in cars that need DOT 4.

With the car parked on level ground and the engine off, unscrew or unsnap the brake reservoir cap(s). Keep it (them) clean. Pour in the fluid until it reaches the "full" line. Replace the cap(s). Since brake

Joel pours brake fluid into a reservoir that is low (arrow). The "full" line (arrow) shows where the fluid should be. The labeled brake fluid reservoir cap sits at the side.

fluid can rust cars and wreck paint, keep it off the car's outside. If some spills, wipe it up right away. Soak any that spills on the ground with cat litter. Clean any that spills on you with soap.

STEERING

Regular steering units turn the front wheels by linking the steering wheel to the wheels with rods and gears. As you turn the steering wheel, your own strength turns the wheels.

Power steering uses a fluid as an actuator. When the steering wheel turns, fluid moves through tubes (lines) and pushes on the power steering unit. It uses power from the engine to make the front wheels turn right or left. Power steering makes turning the steering wheel much easier than nonpower steering units, but if the engine is off, steering becomes very hard with power steering systems.

Many cars today have power steering. Like power brakes, the right amount of power steering fluid must fill the lines. If there's a leak, the power steering unit won't work. Therefore, it's important to make sure that there's enough fluid in the power steering system. Some cars use automatic transmission fluid in the power steering. Check your owner's manual to be sure.

Most power steering units have dipsticks. The owner's manual may picture where the dipstick is, but if not, ask a service station mechanic to point it out. It may be under or attached to a screw cap. Label it with a piece of masking tape and a marker pen so you will not forget its location.

Have the car's owner park it on a level place, off the road. The engine must be off and the parking brake on. Wear old clothes.

The dipstick has marks on it to tell if there's enough fluid. Sometimes it has two marks, one marked H or "hot," the other marked C or "cold." If the car has been running recently, the fluid will be hot and should hit the "hot" mark. If the car has not been running for a while, the fluid will be cold and should hit the "cold" mark. If it falls below the proper mark, you must add more. Be sure to keep the dipstick clean.

If you need to add more fluid, buy power steering fluid at an auto parts or department store. It is always clearly marked and often the same as automatic transmission fluid. Check the owner's manual to make sure.

The power steering unit may have a separate fluid filler cap or you may need to pour fluid into the same hole that the dipstick goes into. Ask a mechanic if you are not sure. If there is a cap, keep it clean. Never overfill the power steering. Extra fluid is wasted. It also makes a mess in the engine compartment.

Nonpower steering fluid is often difficult to check and sometimes requires special tools for adding more. It's best to leave it to a mechanic.

TRANSMISSION

Auto engines run much too fast for slow driving. This is fine for freeways or turnpikes, but engine speed must be reduced for city driving. Giving the engine less gasoline slows it down, but too little gas makes it stall. Auto designers use sets of gears called the transmission to slow down the car's speed while letting the engine run fast enough to keep going. The engine still runs as fast as ever, but the transmission slows down the drive shaft that sends power to the wheels.

Moving transmission gears make friction, which wears them out. Of course, friction can be cut down by lubrication. Since transmissions are complicated and expensive, constant lubrication is important. Therefore, transmission fluid is sealed inside the transmission housing. It bathes all the gears all the time. As long as there's enough fluid (and no racing or crashing), a transmission may last longer than an engine or a car body.

For driving at different speeds, transmissions have different sized gears. A stick shift ("manual") transmission changes gears with a shift lever and clutch. The driver presses the clutch pedal. This disconnects or disengages the transmission from the engine while the driver moves the shift lever to change gears. With the car in gear and the clutch pedal up, the engine and transmission are connected or engaged again.

An automatic transmission changes gears as the gas pedal goes down. It shifts without a clutch pedal, automatically. It might seem silly to have an extra pedal to press when there are automatic transmissions that don't need them. Still, some drivers like stick shift transmissions and clutches. They're cheaper than automatic ones and use less gasoline.

Both automatic and stick shift transmissions need transmission fluid. If there's a leak, the transmission can be ruined by friction and heat. In automatic transmissions, the fluid is an actuator as well as lubricant. The moving fluid helps shift gears just by its movement. Also, in all transmissions, the fluid helps clean and cool the gears. Therefore, in automatic transmissions, transmission fluid lubri-

cates, cleans, cools, and actuates. It does four of the five possible jobs of a fluid in a car. If there's not enough of it, the car and owner are soon in big trouble.

Like power steering units, automatic transmissions have dipsticks. After asking a service station mechanic to point to your automatic transmission dipstick, label it with masking tape and a marking pen. Stick shift transmissions don't have dipsticks. They should be checked and serviced by a mechanic at a service station.

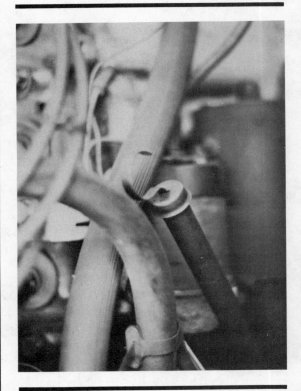

The automatic transmission dipstick in the Chevrolet Vega is at the back of the engine compartment, but looks almost the same as the oil dipstick.

Automatic transmissions sometimes need to have the car engine on in order for their dipsticks to read correctly. Be sure the car is level, off the road, with the parking brake on. If the owner's manual says to, have the driver start the car *in neutral.* TOUCH NO MOVING PARTS. Avoid fans and moving belts. Pull the dipstick out of its tube and wipe it clean with a rag. Stick it back in all the way. Pull it out again and see if the fluid wets the F mark. Keep the dipstick clean and replace it in its tube immediately after checking the fluid level. Turn the car off.

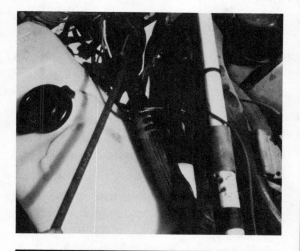

David checks the automatic transmission fluid dipstick. He had to have the car's owner turn the engine on before checking it and was careful not to touch any moving parts. Except for having the car on, checking the transmission fluid dipstick is just like checking the motor oil dipstick.

If more transmission fluid is needed, buy it at an auto parts or department store. Buy the cheapest fluid graded for your car. Special or expensive fluids may not do a better job.

Automatic transmission fluid is always marked for automatic transmissions on the can or bottle. Stick shift transmissions use "gear oil." The container usually says "manual transmission fluid." Never mix up the two. Also, there are different automatic transmission fluids for General Motors and Ford transmissions. General Motors fluid is called "Dexron" and Ford fluid is "Type F." These are *not* the same and must not be confused. If your car is made by another car maker, the owner's manual says which kind of automatic transmission fluid to buy. Always follow its suggestions.

If your car has an automatic transmission fluid filler cap, twist it off and pour in the right amount of fluid. If there's no filler cap, you may have to pour fluid into the dipstick tube. Ask a mechanic if you're not sure. Keep the cap clean and only add fluid up to the "full" line on the dipstick.

A few cars (several Toyota models and possibly others) need fluid in their clutches. That fluid is an actuator and there must be enough of it for the clutch to work properly.

If your car has an extra reservoir under the hood, that may be for clutch fluid. Ask a mechanic and mark the reservoir with tape and a marking pen. If the reservoir is low, add extra fluid—of the proper kind—to it.

All these fluids are bad for auto paint. Wipe up spills right away. Use cat litter to soak up spills on the ground and wash any fluid off yourself with strong soap.

Now every dipstick and reservoir under the hood is marked except for the motor oil dipstick, which you know about, and the radiator. Radiator fluid comes in the next chapter. Meanwhile, you now know what all those little cups of liquid around your engine are for. Next time any one of them gets low, you'll know exactly what to do.

If you like, you can completely change fluids in those reservoirs, too. It can be done at home, but requires more tools. Chapter 18 talks about it.

7. WATER

Difficulty: Easy
Parts: One or two gallons of antifreeze
Water
Window washer fluid
Tools: A clean bucket
2-4 one gallon jugs
Hand soap and/or Pro-Tek (see Ch. 1)
Help needed: None

It would save a lot of trouble if oil cooled a car's engine enough, but it usually doesn't. The Volkswagen Beetle and Chevrolet Corvair had oil and air cooled engines. Most cars don't. Without the water cooling system, most car engines overheat and stop working. Auto designers put a metal case (called a "water jacket") around the hot parts of the car engine. Antifreeze and water flow through the water jacket and the engine heats them. This hot fluid is pumped away from the engine, taking the heat with it. In the radiator, air is fanned past the tubes containing the hot water, cooling it just as a fan cools your face in the summer.

Water is a good fluid for cooling car engines. It's cheap and easy to get—but there are problems with it. The biggest problems show up at 32°F (0°C) and 212°F (100°C). At these temperatures, water freezes and boils—and expands. This means that it takes up more space as ice or steam than it does as liquid water. Of course, there's only a certain amount of room in the cooling system pipes and water jacket. If the water freezes and expands, it can break the pipes and leak out. It may even crack the engine, forcing you to replace the whole thing. To prevent that, antifreeze is added to the radiator water.

Antifreeze is a very poisonous, colorless liquid called ethylene glycol that mixes with water plus some coloring, usually red or green. The color tells you that antifreeze is in the water. Ethylene glycol both lowers the freezing temperature and raises the boiling temperature of water. With enough antifreeze, the water in a car parked outdoors on a cold night won't freeze and crack the engine block. Also, on a hot day, when the car is breezing down the highway, antifreeze keeps the water from boiling and expanding in the radiator. This prevents popping the radiator cap. Since antifreeze works in winter and summer, it's sometimes called an "all-weather cooling system additive" instead of just "antifreeze."

There are also water and antifreeze in the window washer reservoir. In this case, the antifreeze is not ethylene glycol because water that goes on the windows often splashes on the paint. Ethylene glycol ruins paint. Therefore, the antifreeze in the window washer fluid has detergent, like dishwashing detergent, and alcohol in it. There's no high heat in the window washer reservoir, but winter cold may freeze it. The alcohol lowers the freezing temperature of the water and detergent makes it wash the windows a little better.

If there's a leak in the cooling system or if you use the window washers, their water levels may become low. In that case, water *and* antifreeze must be added. The window washer reservoir is usually made of plastic. Look through it to see whether more fluid is needed. The radiator is made of copper. It sits right at the front of the car. To check the fluid level there, remove the radiator cap and look in. If you can't find the radiator cap, ask a mechanic to point to it. If the engine is hot, be careful. Boiling water or steam may shoot out of a hot radiator. Let the car cool before checking. Water should completely cover the metal inside the radiator, which is called the radiator core. The water should be about two inches below the cap when the engine is cold. When the engine is hot, the water will be right up to the top of the radiator.

Be sure you have (1) permission and (2) the proper antifreeze before adding water to the window washer reservoir or the radiator. For the window washers, water, alcohol, and detergent are sold already mixed or you can mix your own. Usually, the already mixed fluid goes on sale at department stores and is the cheapest. Auto parts stores have both mixed and unmixed fluid, but they may be more expensive. Compare prices and buy the cheapest fluid available. Antifreeze for the radiator is sold at department and auto parts stores. Watch for a sale on that, too. Both window washer fluid and cooling system antifreeze are clearly marked with their names. Special brands at high prices are not always good buys.

Have the car's driver park the car on a level surface off the street, with the engine off and the parking brake on. Wear old clothes. Rub a little Pro-Tek on your hands now if you plan to use it on this job.

If your fluid is already mixed, open the window washer cap and pour in the fluid. Close the cap. Be sure not to get any dirt in the fluid because it may clog the window washer pump or the spray jets.

If you bought the unmixed fluid, pour all of it into a clean bucket or large cup. Fill the empty fluid can with water and pour that into the bucket, too. Add one more

Look inside the radiator by taking the cap off. The fluid level in this radiator is low. Fluid should cover the metal "core" inside.

David adds window washer fluid to the reservoir. Many window washer reservoirs are clear so you can see when they are low without opening them.

Joel pours antifreeze and then the same amount of water into a clean bucket.

radiator needs until after you fill it. By then, it's too late. One solution is mixing water and antifreeze in a *clean* bucket before using it. Pour one gallon of antifreeze into a carefully cleaned bucket, then fill the gallon jug with water and pour that into the bucket. Use the mixture in the bucket to fill the radiator. If that's not enough, mix up another gallon of antifreeze and water and fill the radiator.

Any left over must be stored in a container (or two) that can be closed to keep the mixture clean. The empty antifreeze jug(s) can hold some, and an old, clean milk or cider bottle can hold the rest. Be sure to have the extra jug(s) ready before mixing the water and antifreeze. Label the jugs "mixed antifreeze."

Fill the radiator to two or three inches from the top. Fluid must cover the radiator core, but never fill it all the way up to the cap. When the engine gets hot, a full radi-

can of water and stir. Pour as much of this mixture as needed into the window washer reservoir. Save the rest in a clean, tightly closed, clearly marked bottle. Again, be sure no dirt gets into the reservoir to clog the washer jets.

The radiator's fluid is like the unmixed window washer fluid. For most of the country, you need half water and half antifreeze. Most antifreeze jugs explain how much water and antifreeze to mix. Check the back of the jug. Unfortunately, it's impossible to know how much fluid the

Again using the kitchen cup, Joel fills the radiator. The cup isn't required, but it makes it easy to pour without spilling. Wash it carefully before replacing it in the kitchen.

ator may overflow. Don't spill any water and antifreeze mixture when adding it to the radiator. This is important because ethylene glycol attacks auto paint. Wash off any spills. Also be sure to keep the radiator cap clean while it's off the radiator. Replace it as soon as you're finished filling up. When you're done, wash the floor. This is easiest if you did the job outside and can wash with a garden hose.

Usually, auto makers say you should change all your cooling system fluid once every other year. This isn't a hard job. Gasoline stations charge more to do it than you do. Chapter 18 has information about it.

Since some antifreeze and water was spilled, Joel washes the area with a garden hose. This washes the antifreeze away and dilutes it.

Using a kitchen measuring cup, Joel pours the antifreeze and water mixture back into the jug to save it for use another time.

8. BATTERIES

Difficulty: Easy
Parts: Distilled water
Tools: Plastic goggles to protect eyes
from acid
Help needed: None

Cars use batteries. They're heavy black boxes—not the little dry cells in toys and flashlights. When cars were first invented, they did not have batteries. People had to start them by turning a crank on the front. You can still see some of these old cars in museums and movies. Now, the battery gives electricity to an electric motor (called a "starter"), which starts the engine at the turn of a key. Since turning the crank to start a car took a lot of strength, electric starters are a big improvement.

Auto batteries are called "wet cells" because they have liquid inside them. The round batteries in toys are dry cells, with almost no liquid. Wet cells store much larger amounts of electrical power than

dry cells. Since starting a car takes a lot of current, wet cells are needed.

Inside a wet cell battery are lead plates. Between the plates is a special liquid called an electrolyte. The electrolyte allows electricity to flow through it from

Here are four batteries. The little D cell is used in flashlights, radios, and toys. The big battery with no caps on top is a maintenance-free battery. The others are an old and a new auto battery to which water must be added now and then. Arrow A points to the battery caps and arrow B points out where the month and year the battery was bought are shown.

Every battery has terminals for positive (+) and negative (-). Arrow C points to those terminals on the maintenance-free battery.

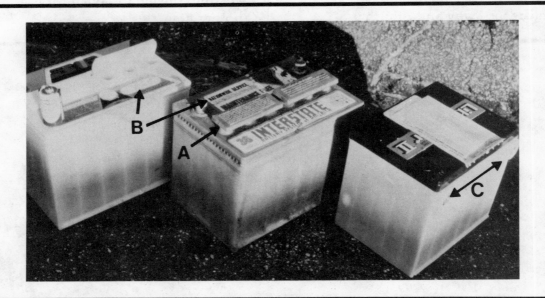

one plate to another. In auto batteries, the electrolyte is water and sulfuric acid.

When the engine is turned off, tiny electrons move through the electrolyte to the plates connected to the negative(-) battery post. The post then has too many electrons. The plates connected to the positive (+) post have too few.

This is a schematic of a car's ignition and starting system. The parallel lines in the middle of **A** and **B** are symbols for car batteries. The circle with a broken line inside it to the batteries' left stands for a key or ignition switch next to the steering wheel. The lines connecting each part are wires. Both **A** and **B** show the switches in their "Off" position.

The key switch has several positions. Drawing **A** shows what's in the circuit when the switch is "On." Electricity flows (follow the arrowheads) from the negative battery terminal through the switch and into the spark plugs and voltage regulator. It continues through the alternator and back to the positive battery terminal. Still the car won't start.

The key must be turned to "Start" (**B**) so the starter can turn on the engine. When that's done, everything in **A** and **B** is in the circuit. The spark plugs fire and the alternator produces current. Once the engine starts, a spring in the key switch pushes the key back from "Start" to "On" so the starter no longer runs. It isn't needed with the engine running.

When the driver turns the ignition key, those extra electrons flow from the negative post through all the wires and the starter motor to the positive post. This flow is called electricity. As long as the battery is in good condition, enough electricity flows and the car starts.

Diagram of Ignition

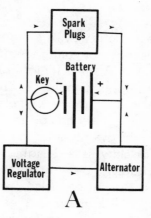

A

and Starting System

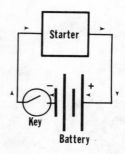

B

31

To keep more electrons at the negative post than at the positive one, cars have a built-in charging system. The alternator and voltage regulator automatically recharge the battery as the engine runs. If (1) they work properly, (2) the battery isn't worn out, and (3) there's enough water in it, the battery will take and hold its charge. Holding that charge is also called storing electricity. Since these batteries store electricity, they are sometimes called "storage batteries."

There are four ways a battery may fail. (1) The alternator or voltage regulator may break down. A mechanic must check these with special tools. (2) The battery may wear out. That usually takes several years. Every battery has printed on it how many months (twenty-four, thirty-six, forty-eight, or sixty) it is designed for, but it may last much longer and still start the car. If it does, be happy. Also be ready to replace it. (3) If someone leaves the headlights or other lights on for a long time when the engine is off, the battery will supply current to those lights until it runs out. When that happens, the battery is dead. Fortunately, a gasoline station can recharge the battery if you take it there. (4) Finally, water may evaporate from the battery.

You can solve the last problem yourself in most batteries by adding water. Look at the top of the plastic box under the hood. If you can't find it, ask a mechanic to point it out. It's the battery and there should be heavy wires coming from each side of it. On top, find two lines of holes, covered with caps. If there are no holes or caps, you have a "maintenance free" battery. Add no water to it. If there are holes, their caps are together in groups of three. Pull the caps off, keeping them clean, and look inside each hole. The water inside is mixed with sulfuric acid. DO NOT TOUCH IT! It will burn you. If the water covers all the metal plates, you have enough water. If not, in one or more cells, add some.

The battery needs more water in it. The plates inside the cell are uncovered.

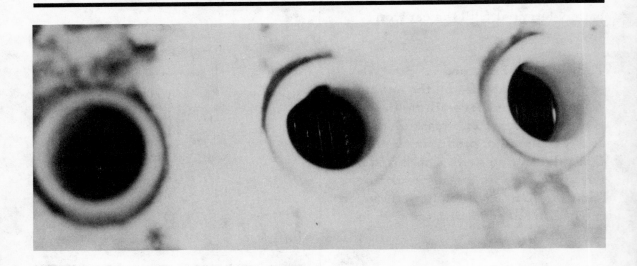

The acid in automotive storage batteries is strong. Splashed on clothes, it will burn neat round holes in them wherever it lands. It takes ten to twenty minutes to burn those holes, but they appear. On skin, it burns in only a few minutes. A single

David adds distilled water to the low battery cells. He put water in a kitchen measuring cup to help prevent spills.

Never **overfill a battery with water. Overfilling may spill acid on the car and damage it. Acid can also hurt you if it gets on your skin.**

drop in your eyes may blind you. Therefore, be careful with batteries! Do *not* splash acid. If some does splash on clothes, wash them with water and baking soda right away. The baking soda will neutralize the acid so it doesn't ruin your clothes. If some gets on your skin, wash with lots and lots of water. Baking soda will help, too. It is a good idea to wear plastic goggles to protect your eyes from splashed acid, but if you accidentally do get some in your eyes, put them under running water from a hose or tap. Open your eyes and let the water wash them. Have someone else call the hospital or emergency squad. Keep washing your eyes until help comes. The

best way to avoid problems is to be careful not to splash any acid in the first place.

Batteries never need acid added, only water. Before adding water, be sure you have the right kind. Water from a garden hose or tap isn't the best for batteries because, besides water, it has chemicals in it. Batteries are finicky. They want pure water. Supermarkets and drugstores sell gallon jugs of distilled water for steam irons and car batteries. They cost about one dollar for one gallon, which lasts a long time.

Carefully pour your distilled water into the cell that is low. Make sure water covers the plates inside, but don't fill it to the top. Too much water will splash out of the battery even with the caps on. That water, remember, is mixed with acid. Acid can eat away the steel of the car. If you do spill some distilled water from the jug, don't worry. Distilled water can't hurt anything inside the engine compartment. Be sure to snap the battery caps on firmly after adding the water. Always keep them clean.

Some batteries have no caps; they are completely sealed so they don't need water. They are also the most expensive batteries available, but they can still wear out. (These batteries' makers usually guarantee them until the car is sold.) It's easy and cheap to add water now and then. Now that you know how, when battery replacement time comes, your parents or other car owner might want to consider buying the cheaper batteries.

One final word of caution. Never let anyone smoke or light matches near a battery. In order to make electricity, car batteries also make a highly explosive gas called hydrogen. Car batteries may explode if a flame or spark comes too close to them.

9. BATTERY ACID

Difficulty: Moderate
Parts: Battery terminal
protective washers or spray (optional)
(for example, No-Co from Sears)
Tools: Baking soda
Open end wrenches
Screwdriver
Masking tape
Marker pen
Two cement blocks
Coarse steel wool
Garden hose and water
Small plastic dish
Rags
Hand soap and/or Pro-Tek (see Ch. 1)
Help needed: One adult

Batteries have acid in them, produce explosive hydrogen gas, and supply electricity, but they aren't as dangerous as they sound. The electricity can hurt when the engine is running and you foolishly touch the ignition terminals. With the engine off, shocks are unlikely even if you try to get them. Picking up the battery (*without* dropping or spilling it) isn't dangerous. It's not a bomb. There is no explosion danger if you avoid sparks or flames. Besides, gasoline in the gas tank is no less dangerous than the hydrogen. The only problem is the acid and that is dangerous. A little on your skin hurts, but you wash it off (fast!) with lots of water. Acid spilled on the car should be washed off at once.

Since a car is made of steel, you might think that acid would hurt your skin more than the car. This would be true except that cars are very stupid. If a drop of acid spills on your hand, you wash it off. A car doesn't. It doesn't even ask *you* to wash the acid off. It just sits there.

Sometimes, the best batteries splash acid through the little holes in the top of the battery caps. Those holes let hydrogen gas out so that it doesn't build up and burst the battery. Unfortunately, they also give off an acid mist. Since cars never complain, you might not know something bad has happened unless you check.

Do this job with the car parked on a level driveway or parking lot. Never work on a car parked in the street. Have the parking brake on, the engine off, and wear old clothes. Since this is a messy job, it's a good time to try Pro-Tek, the protective hand cream, if you haven't already. Put it on now.

Look at your battery where the wires attach to the terminals. The things that attach the wires to the terminals are called battery terminal clamps. They're sometimes covered with a greenish-blue, fuzzy material. That is lead sulfate, a kind of rust. The word "rust" usually applies to steel or iron. Iron rust is brown and crumbly, but lead "rust" is greenish-blue.

Lead sulfate conducts electricity poorly. If too much builds up on the battery terminals, it can stop current from reaching the starter or other electrical parts. You might think the battery is dead when the terminals only need cleaning.

Worse, if acid splashes down the battery's sides, it can eat away the shelf on which the battery sits. To check if this has happened, you must remove the battery. First, loosen (but do *not* remove) the nuts that hold the clamps to the battery terminals. Use a small open end wrench. Open end wrenches come in sets at department stores or auto parts stores. The whole set has many useful sized wrenches in it for

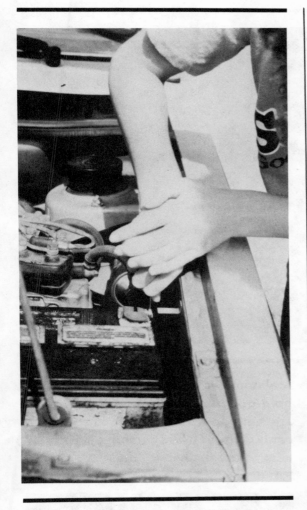

When the nuts are loose, notice where each wire is attached, then carefully turn the terminal clamps from one side to the other. Do *not* grab the clamps with a pliers and pull. You could pull the battery terminal completely off. Then you would have to buy a new battery. If the clamp doesn't turn, carefully spread the clamp jaws with an old screwdriver. Don't snap off the battery terminal. Once the terminal clamp is loose, gently work it from side to side, pulling up. The clamp and attached wires will come off in your hand. Wrap masking tape around all the wires that were connected to the positive battery terminal. Look carefully: the positive terminal is labeled "+" or "pos." Write a plus (+) on the tape with a marker pen. Wrap masking tape around the wires from the negative ("-" or "neg") terminal. Mark that tape with a minus(-). Push all the taped, labeled wires out of the way of the battery.

Ali loosens the battery terminal clamp nut on a corroded terminal.
Sometimes, this nut can be very tight or corroded on. If you can't turn it, ask an adult for help. You may need some penetrating oil (see Chapter 15).

about ten or twelve dollars. It'll last the rest of your life if you take care of it. Be sure to buy metric system (millimeters) wrenches if your car is metric, or English system (inches) wrenches if your car uses English system nuts and bolts. The owner's manual tells you which you have.

She twists the clamp from side to side and pulls up at the same time.
Sometimes clamps are very tight. An adult may need to help. Be careful not to snap off the terminal. Once the clamps are off, clean them with a wire brush.

Remember which wire is positive (+) and which is negative (-) when putting them back on.

Unscrew or unhook any battery "hold-downs" that hold the battery. These may be holding the sides or come over the top of the battery. Some cars have none at all. Don't lose the hold-downs. Put them aside.

Now, since batteries are heavy (twenty or more pounds), you need help. Tell a strong adult that the job is easy and only takes a minute or two. Don't try to do it yourself. Dropping a battery spills acid and may crack the battery itself. New batteries cost forty or fifty dollars. Therefore, don't break the one you have.

Before your helper picks the battery up, make a little stand out of cement blocks or bricks in the driveway or parking lot. Then, ask your helper to lift the battery out of the car. Keep it straight up so no acid spills. Reread page 33 for what to do about spilled acid. The main thing is, do *not* spill any. Place the battery on the stand you made.

Joel removes one side of the battery hold-down on another battery. There are many kinds of hold-downs; each car is different. Only remove what you must to get the battery out.

An adult places the battery on a cement block stand. Space under the battery lets you clean its bottom. Do not tip the battery. Acid mustn't spill.

Look at the shelf that held the battery. Some are plastic. They can't rust, but if the car is more than two or three years old, that shelf is probably made of steel. It may be rusty and the rust is no regular rust, either. It's acid rust. There's usually no way that water can get underneath a battery in a car, but splashed acid can get there. It does more damage than a whole lake.

If the shelf is rusty or there's lead sulfate on the battery terminals, you can clean them as well as any garage or service station. You don't take short cuts or scrimp on time.

Remove the rusty battery shelf with your wrenches by taking out the bolts that hold it. Save the bolts and any washers under them. If you can't get the shelf out, clean it in the car. However, removing it is better. With the shelf out, you can clean under it.

The easiest way to remove dirt fast is to spray water on the shelf and battery with a hose. Make sure the battery's caps are on tight before hosing it down.

David and Joel clean the battery and its shelf with steel wool. The bolts and washers that held the shelf are soaking in the cup of kerosene. Keep kerosene away from the battery terminals and caps.

David turns a bolt with an open end wrench to remove the battery shelf. It's badly rusted.

Make sure the battery caps are tight, then wash the shelf and battery with water. Water from a hose won't hurt the battery's outsides. If there's a lot of grease or dirt on the battery or shelf, use coarse steel wool to scrub it off. Throw the steel wool away when you're done. This may be a long job, but don't give up. Clean the battery bottom, too, *without* turning the battery over. Soap is good for the shelf, if necessary, but be careful *not* to get soap through the battery cap holes. It'll ruin the battery's insides. Clean under the battery shelf.

You may want to buy a special tool for cleaning battery terminals and clamps. Several work, but steel wool is cheaper and works just as well. When cleaning the terminals: do *not* use soap. Water is fine. By the way, mechanics use those special tools for cleaning battery terminals and clamps because they're fast. Mechanics rarely remove batteries or shelves for cleaning because it takes too long.

Your battery, terminals, clamps, and shelf still aren't clean. They look clean, but there's still some acid on them. It'll slowly eat the steel if you don't stop it. The magic acid killer is sold in supermarkets and is very cheap. It's baking soda. Buy a box for your car or borrow some from the kitchen.

In a plastic dish, mix a handful of baking soda with water. It should feel like slightly watery paste. Smear the paste over the rusty parts of the shelf, the clamps, and most of the battery. Never put any on the battery terminals or caps. It'll *wreck* the battery's insides. If you look carefully, you can see tiny bubbles in the soda and water mixture when it hits metal rusted by acid. If you can't see them, put your ear near the battery or shelf and listen to them fizz. That's the soda neutralizing the acid, making carbon dioxide bubbles. Be sure to

David and Joel smear baking soda paste on the shelf to neutralize any leftover acid.

clean the shelf screws or bolts and battery hold-downs in the soda paste, too.

After the baking soda sits on everything for fifteen or twenty minutes, all the acid should be gone. Wash the soda away with water. Make very sure NO soda gets inside the battery. Put the shelf back and tighten its bolts or screws with a wrench or screwdriver.

Before having your strong helper replace the battery, put a little dry baking soda on the shelf. The battery can sit in baking soda and, if acid spills, the soda will neutralize it. The shelf may still rust, but it'll rust more slowly than it would have if it weren't cleaned. Some battery shelves are never cleaned. They sometimes rust away so that the battery falls out of the car. Yours won't do that.

Optional super-special touch: If you want to, get some felt battery terminal protective washers or a can of "No-Co" or other electrical system anti-corrosion spray at an auto parts store. "Corrosion" is the

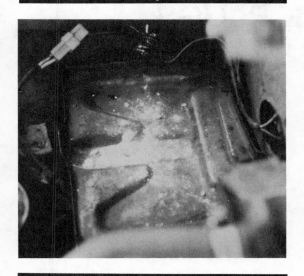

Joel sprinkles baking soda on the battery shelf. It neutralizes acid that may spill there in the future.

chemical word for rust. One can costs three or four dollars. Two washers cost a dollar or two. The cans last many years, but the washers only last one year. These chemicals, like baking soda, neutralize acid. They also make a better electrical connection between the wires and battery. Spray *a little* (not too much) on the battery terminals or place one washer on each terminal. Then slide the clamps back on the proper (+ or -) terminals and tighten the nuts with a wrench. (Note: you may replace the clamps without the anticorrosion washers or spray. Most mechanics do.) Tighten the clamps' nuts firmly, but *not* as hard as you can. If there are battery hold-downs, put them back and tighten them.

You've cleaned your battery, terminals, clamps, and shelf as well as the best mechanic would. It cost very little (much less than replacing a battery shelf) and makes the car last longer and run better. The job needs doing about once a year, but it'll be easier next time.

Wash your hands and try for a raise in your allowance.

Joel sprays anticorrosion spray on the clean battery terminal. A little goes a long way. Anticorrosion washers are neater, but only last one year. A can of spray lasts many years.

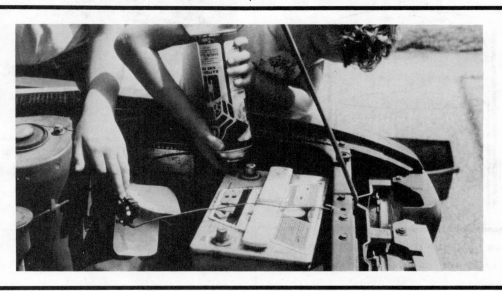

10. SPARK PLUGS

Difficulty: Moderate
Parts: New spark plugs
Tools: Spark plug wrench or
Socket wrench set with spark plug socket
Spark plug gap gauge
Torque wrench with adaptor
for above sockets
Hand soap and/or Pro-Tek (see Ch. 1)
Help needed: None

More than a thousand times every minute, gasoline explodes in a running car engine. Then, the rods, pistons, shafts, and gears turn the explosions' force into movement. Since gasoline cannot burn by itself, it is mixed with air in the carburetor, but that still isn't enough. Gasoline and air need high heat to set them off. Spark plugs, the heart of an auto's engine, light the fire.

It's no ordinary fire, either. Before the gasoline and air explode, their temperature is between 850°F and 1,500°F. They explode when as much as 20,000 volts of electricity jump across the plug's spark gap. At the spark, the temperature is several thousand degrees Fahrenheit. (When regular paper burns, the beginning temperature is 451°F.) All this happens, remember, millions and millions of times during a car's life.

The high temperatures and voltages at the tip of a spark plug shorten its life. In the air from the carburetor, there's often a small amount of water vapor. That vapor, harmless at normal temperatures, can rust steel at several thousand degrees. Also, tiny amounts of oil leak into the cylinder where the explosions take place. That oil

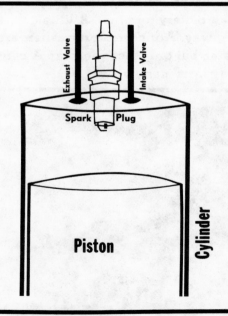

A spark plug fits into each cylinder next to the valves and above the piston.

David holds a new spark plug in his left hand and an old, gummy one in his right. The old plug is from an engine that was leaking oil into the cylinder. You can tell because it's black. An old spark plug from a properly running engine is light tan or gray.

burns poorly. It leaves a black, gummy material on the spark plugs. Plugs fouled with gum, rust, or other things from a car's engine don't work properly. In time, these deposits prevent the spark from burning all the gasoline and air. Sometimes, the fouling keeps the plugs from firing at all. When that happens the gasoline in the cylinder is wasted.

Like motor oil, air filters, and oil filters, spark plugs should be changed. Check the odometer, the sticker on the side of the driver's door, and the owner's manual—or ask the car's owner—to tell you when to change spark plugs. Subtract the sticker number (when the plugs were last changed) from the odometer reading. The remainder is the number of miles the car has gone since changing plugs. Some cars can go 6,000 miles between spark plug changes. Some go 12,000 miles and some even manage 24,000 miles between plug changes. The owner's manual says how many miles your car should go between spark plug changes.

If it's time to change plugs, you can do it. Changing your own spark plugs saves a lot of money and time. You also get to see what the end of a spark plug looks like after it's lived through millions of explosions. Most important, your car will run better and use less gasoline. New spark plugs always make gasoline burn cleaner, hotter, and faster than old ones.

After checking with the car's owner to make sure it's all right for you to change the plugs, go to an auto parts or department store and buy new plugs. They cost $1.00 to $1.30 each. You need one spark plug for each cylinder and should change all of them at the same time. The owner's manual says how many cylinders there are. It also tells the car's make, model, and year. You may need (from the manual) the engine size. Check the spark plug chart at the department store to get the right plug number or ask the counter person at the auto parts store for plugs to match your car. Sometimes, spark plugs are on sale. Buy the cheapest ones available. All spark plugs made for your car work.

A spark plug wrench is needed to remove and replace plugs. This wrench looks like a tube about two or three inches long. They're sold separately (about five

A spark plug wrench is on the left. In the middle are two spark plug sockets. A socket works with a socket wrench handle (right). The square drive pin on the handle fits into the square hole in the socket.

dollars) or in a set of socket wrenches in the same stores that sell spark plugs. If you or the car's owner can afford a socket set, buy it. The three-eighths inch drive size is best for general home and auto repairs. Be careful to buy slightly better than the very cheapest set because the cheapest ones may be poorly chrome plated. If you use them a lot, the chrome may peel off and the sockets rust. Good sockets last a lifetime. Many companies make good socket sets, but some of the better ones are Snap-On, S-K, Truecraft, Blackhawk, and Sears Craftsman. Snap-On tools are often more expensive than the others. Get metric sockets if your car is metric, English system sockets if your car's nuts and bolts are measured in inches.

The tops of spark plugs, like good dishes, are made of ceramic. They are delicate. Therefore, be careful screwing plugs into their holes. A torque wrench

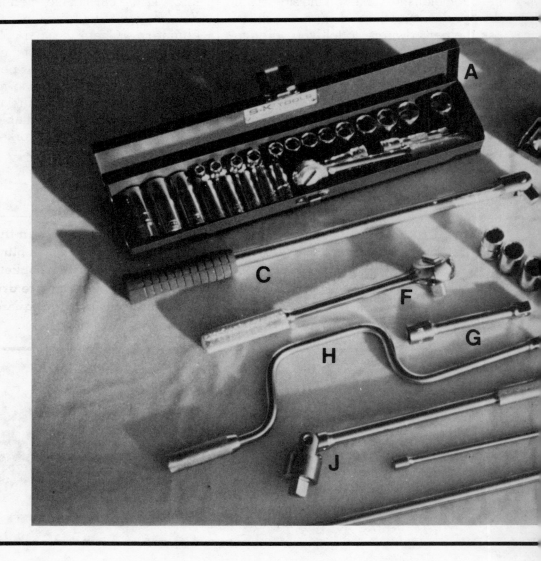

measures the force used to turn things. It warns you if you tighten too much. Therefore, it's a good tool to own for replacing spark plugs.

There are three types of torque wrenches: (1) beam, (2) dial, and (3) micrometer. The first is the cheapest and, some mechanics say, the best. It never goes out of adjustment like the others. The dial and micrometer torque wrenches are for professionals only. A beam torque wrench costs about twelve to fifteen dollars. If you can afford one, buy one that measures from five to one hundred fifty foot-pounds with a one-half-inch drive size. Also, get (about one dollar) a one-half-inch to three-eighths-inch adaptor for your three-eighths-inch drive spark plug socket. Since a torque wrench is good for changing tires (Chapter 15), replacing gaskets (Chapter 17), and other auto repairs, it's a good tool to own. Since torque wrenches use socket

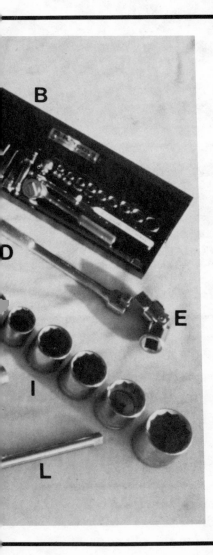

Socket wrenches have many parts. Some are necessary, others are only needed for special jobs. Sizes (1/4", 3/8", 1/2") refer to the length of a side of the square drive pin on the handle or the square hole on each socket.

A. 3/8" socket wrench set, includes sockets and handle
B. 1/4" socket wrench set, includes sockets and handle
C. 3/8" breaker bar for loosening very tight nuts or bolts
D. 3/8" medium length extension for hard to reach nuts and bolts
E. 3/8" universal joint for reaching around corners
F. 1/2" ratchet handle
G. 3/8" short extension
H. 1/2" speeder handle for putting in many nuts or bolts quickly
I. 1/2" socket set (handle doesn't come with these sockets)
J. 1/2" breaker bar
K. 3/8" medium length extension
L. 3/8" long extension

For most work, all you need is a 3/8" socket wrench set. Buy other things as you need them.

At right is an in-line, four cylinder engine. Arrows point out its spark plugs. In the center is a slant-six engine. Its spark plugs are also indicated with arrows. The V-8 engine's spark plugs (below right) are not visible from above. They are located below other parts and are hard to see and reach. If you can't find the plugs in your car, ask a mechanic.

wrench sockets, don't buy one if you don't own a socket set. If you can't afford a torque wrench, you can still change spark plugs. You must, however, be extra careful tightening new ones.

Make sure the engine is off. The car must be parked on level ground. If it's been running, let it cool off for one hour or you may burn yourself on the hot spark plugs. Set the parking brake. Wear old clothes. If you plan to use it, now is the time to smear on Pro-Tek.

Spark plugs fit in holes on the top or sides of the engine. Wires snap to their tops. If you can't find them, ask a gas station mechanic to point at them. Grab the first wire just above the plug and carefully pull. It should come off with a moderate tug. Do *not* pull the wires off all the plugs at once. You might mix them up. Each wire goes to a specific plug. Remove the wire, then the plug, then replace that plug and put the wire back. To remove the spark plug, place your spark plug wrench on the plug, put on the wrench handle, and twist the plug loose. Be careful not to strike any spark plug with anything hard. Spark plugs can break and bits of ceramic may get inside the engine. Ceramic bits can scratch and ruin a good engine. After unscrewing it from the engine, remove the old plug from the wrench or socket.

Ali pulls a spark plug wire off. The arrow shows that she's careful to pull straight away from the plug.

Before putting new spark plugs into the engine, they must be "gapped." At the bottom of each spark plug is a little bump and a bent piece of steel that looks like a finger asking you to come closer. The bump and the bent steel are called electrodes. When the engine is running, a high voltage spark jumps between the electrodes, lighting the gasoline and air in the cylinder. The exact distance between the electrodes is important for the engine to run well. Usually, that space is carefully measured and set at the spark plug factory. Sometimes, it may be off and you must check and correct it.

The correct distance or "gap" between the electrodes is given in thousandths of an inch and in hundredths of a millimeter. For example, .030" is thirty-thousandths of an inch. It is also the same as .76mm which is seventy-six hundredths of a millimeter.

After removing the plug wire, she takes the plug out with a spark plug socket and socket wrench handle. When removing the plug, always turn counterclockwise. Replace the plug by screwing clockwise.

Your owner's manual tells exactly what the spark gap should be. Usually, there's a range of good settings. For example, the manual may say that the spark gap should be .028-.032" which is the same as .71mm-.81mm.

To measure the spark gap and change it, if necessary, buy a spark gap gauge. They're sold in department and auto parts stores from about seventy-five cents and up. The simplest have several wires sticking out of them. Each wire is a different thickness and all are marked. Find the wire whose thickness is as close as possible to what the manual says is the proper distance between the electrodes.

Put a new spark plug into the spark plug wrench. If there's a plastic or cardboard cover on any part of the new plug, remove it. The electrodes should be sticking out the bottom of the plug wrench. If they're not, you put the spark plug into the wrench upside down. Reverse it.

Try to pass the spark plug gap gauge wire of the proper thickness between the new plug's electrodes. If it won't fit, the gap is too small. If it will fit, try to put the next thicker wire between the electrodes. If that fits, too, the gap is too big. If the proper wire just barely fits, perfect.

At the side of the gap gauge is a slot. This is for adjusting the gap. Put the curved part of the bent wire electrode into the slot of the gauge. Very *carefully* bend the electrode to make the spark bigger or smaller, as necessary. Since you only need to change the gap by a few thousandths of an inch, very little bending is needed. If you bend it too much, the electrode may break off, and the spark plug will be ruined. So, be careful. Now try the spark gap wires again. Perhaps you have bent too much and the gap is now too large when it was too small before or *vice versa*. If so, reverse the process and bend the other way. Keep bending very slightly and trying the correct spark gap wires until your spark gap is within the manual's correct range. Remember, too large or too small a gap and the engine will run poorly. The proper spark gap gives the best gasoline mileage and the most power.

Now screw the new, properly gapped spark plug, and the washers that came with it, in place. Do not grab the plug wrench's or socket wrench's handle. Turn the socket itself with your hands and make

David measures the spark gap on a new spark plug with a gap gauge. The little wires sticking out of the gauge are carefully measured for thickness. The wire that has the same thickness as the proper gap is the one he wants to fit—no bigger.

After measuring the spark gap, David has to bend the electrode to make it slightly bigger. He uses the slot on the side of the spark plug gap gauge to help bend. The arrow shows which direction to bend for making the gap bigger. When doing this, be very careful. Bending too much can snap the electrode off. That ruins the spark plug.

sure you screw it in straight. Don't let the threads bind or the plug could be ruined. Worse, the threads in the hole might be ruined. That's expensive to fix.

When the new plug gets hard to turn, put the torque wrench on the spark plug socket and turn it slowly until the pointer says eleven or twelve foot-pounds. That will not seem very tight, but it's tight enough. Do *not* overtighten spark plugs. Remove the wrench and push the spark plug wire *very firmly* onto the top of the new plug. Do the same to each spark plug in order.

If you have no torque wrench, tighten each spark plug with your plug wrench. After the plug gets too hard to turn with your hands, turn it about one-half to three-quarters of a turn more with the wrench. *Never* tighten spark plugs as hard as you can with a wrench. If a tight spark plug breaks, you will have more problems than you ever want to see.

Look carefully at the old spark plugs. If your engine hasn't been running well, Chapter 18 talks about how to figure out what might be wrong with it by looking at the old spark plugs. Garage mechanics are impressed with people who tell *them* what's wrong with their own car. The old plugs may tell the tale.

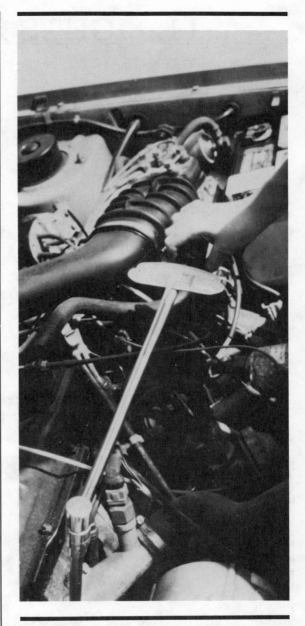

Ali tightens the spark plug into its hole in the engine with a torque wrench. The pointer on the wrench points at twelve (12) foot-pounds which is the correct torque for spark plugs. All plugs should be tightened the same amount.

11. LIGHTS AND FUSES

Difficulty: Moderate
Parts: New Light bulbs
New fuses
Tools: Screwdriver
Flashlight or Troublelight
Hand soap and/or Pro-Tek (see Ch. 1)
Help needed: None

What do you do when a light goes out at home? How about when all the lights in one room go out? How about when *all* the lights go out? Figuring out what is wrong from a little evidence is troubleshooting. Doctors, detectives, and auto mechanics do it—and so can you.

Troubleshooters actually guess at the most likely thing wrong. They are not always right, but good ones usually are. If one light at home—or in a car—dies, the bulb is probably burned out or broken. Replace the bulb and the light usually returns. Usually. Some-

times the socket or the wires are broken, but that's rare. Always shoot for the most likely solution first.

All a car's or room's bulbs do not burn out at once. If all the lights go out, the electricity must have been cut off. A wire might have broken, but that's not likely. Since all current for a group of lights goes through one fuse, the fuse might have burned out. Checking the fuses takes a moment and replacing one is a snap. If the lights return, that's it.

Just as all the lights never blow at once, neither do the fuses. If all the lights go, the

Joel is holding different auto light bulbs in his right hand and fuses in his left. Different cars take different kinds of lights and fuses. Ask for the same kind that are in your car at the auto parts store when replacing any.

electricity is off. At home, call the electric company. For the car, a service station's special tools must check the battery. It may need recharging or replacing. Some wire might be broken or the alternator or voltage regulator might be dead.

LIGHTS

Now that the troubleshooting is done, you must fix the car. A burned out or broken headlight is easy because *you* don't fix it at all. Some headlights need special tools to replace them. Some must be aimed. All service stations replace them in a few minutes and many only charge about one dollar more than the list price of the bulb. Take your car with the broken headlight to a service station.

For replacing lights, be sure the engine is off. Set the parking brake. Wear old clothes because the bulbs are not the only parts that you will touch.

Parking lights (white ones in front), tail and brake lights (red in back), back-up lights (white in back), and running lights (amber on the sides) are usually easy to replace. First, the bulbs aren't usually different colors. They are usually clear. The colors come from colored covers that must be removed to reach the bulbs. Most covers are held on by two small screws.

Remove the screws with a screwdriver and take them off. You may need a Phillips-head screwdriver. There's often a rubber gasket under the sides of the cover. Be careful of it. It prevents water from hitting a hot bulb and cracking it. Save the screws, cover, and gasket.

Most bulbs fit into bayonet sockets. Push the bulb toward the socket and turn it a little. It'll come out easily. Take the dead bulb to an auto parts store and ask for a replacement. They usually cost less than one dollar. Push and turn the new bulb into the socket, replace the gasket, and screw down the cover.

David removes the bulb from its bayonet socket. To do this he must push the bulb *toward* the socket and twist it about one-quarter of a turn. The arrows show how to turn it.

David uses a Phillips-head screwdriver to remove the light cover from a burned-out light. The Phillips-head screwdriver has a cross instead of a straight blade. Phillips-head screws need this special tool.
The arrow points to one gasket under the light cover. There's another inside the cover. They keep water and dirt out. Don't lose the gaskets.

Some lights are replaced from the inside of the trunk or engine compartment. The colored cover isn't removed from these bulbs. In fact, the whole socket, with the bulb still in it and its wires attached, comes out from the inside of the car. Some sockets only need to be pulled to remove them. Others must be turned and pulled at the same time. Once the socket is out, take out the bulb and replace it the same way as the ones with the removable covers.

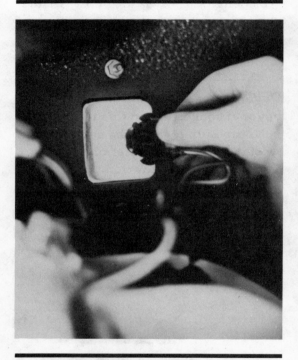

Joel removes the wires from a light inside the trunk. He turns the plastic cap with its wires about one-eighth of a turn clockwise to remove it. Inside, the light bulb is in a bayonet socket.

The bulb on the ceiling is also replaceable. Pull, unscrew, or slide the plastic cover off. Remove the bulb and get a new one.

The only lights you can't replace are ones that need bumper removal.

If your car has such lights, take it to a service station. They charge a lot to replace the burned-out bulbs because it's a big job. Remind your parents of that when they buy a new car.

FUSES

For replacing fuses, the engine must be off. Have it parked on a level place with the parking brake on. Wear old clothes.

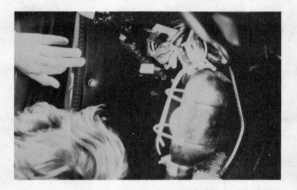

David lies on the floor of the car to look at the fuseblock. Next to him, hanging from a hook, is his troublelight.

Never work on any car that's parked in the street.

If all the running lights or both head-lights go out, suspect a fuse. In fact, if any two or more electrical devices in a car fail, suspect a fuse. The "fuseblock" holds all the fuses under the dashboard. Lie down on the driver's floor and find the fuseblock. It may have a plastic cover. If so, snap it off. The fuses are little glass tubes with wires inside. Check each carefully with a flashlight or troublelight. (A trouble-light is a regular light bulb inside a wire cage at the end of an extension cord. They are sold at department or auto parts stores for eight to twelve dollars each. Some are more expensive because their extension cords are long. Buy the cheapest one you can get.) When checking the fuses, look for one with a broken wire inside the glass tube. A broken wire means a burned fuse.

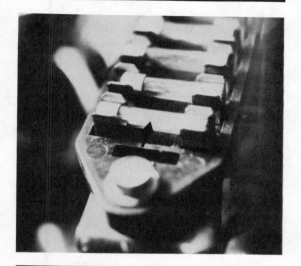

In the fuseblock, the first fuse is burned out. All the others are still good. The burned-out one has a melted piece of wire in its center (arrow).

A plastic auto fuse puller costs about one dollar at an auto parts store, but you can remove fuses with your hands and, if necessary, a screwdriver. Be careful not to break the fuse because the broken glass can cut you.

Take the burned-out fuse to the auto parts store and buy a new one like it. Fuses have different current ratings that are printed on the fuse; 10A, 15A, and 20A are standard ratings for auto fuses. Always replace a fuse with a new one of the *same* rating. Snap the new fuse into its space with your hands and replace the fuse-block cover, if there was one.

On the right, David removes a burned fuse with a screwdriver. He carefully pries out the fuse, without breaking it. On the left, he uses a fuse puller. They cost about one dollar and make the job easier, but fuses don't burn out very often. A screwdriver does just as well.

Turn on the engine and turn on the light or other electrical device that didn't work before. If it works now, great. If not, check the fuses again. If the new fuse is burned out (broken wire inside), don't replace it until the reason for the burn-out is found and fixed.

Fuses are safety devices. If something is wrong with the electrical system, they burn out before something more expensive is ruined or starts a fire. If a fuse burns out twice in a row, have the owner take the car to a service station or, better, a dealer who sells that kind of new car. Electrical system problems are sometimes complicated and service stations may not be able to do the job. The new car dealer's service department will have the equipment and knowledge to fix the problem.

After the electrical problem is fixed, you can replace the fuse yourself. Remember, fuses are safety devices. Never put a higher-rated fuse in a low-rated fuse holder. You could start a fire. It isn't worth the risk.

12. HOSES AND TUBES

Difficulty: Moderate
Parts: New hoses
Two hose clamps per hose
Water and antifreeze mixture
Tools: Flashlight or Troublelight
Screwdriver
Sharp knife
Pliers
Coarse steel wool
Rags
Tub for catching radiator fluid
Hand soap and/or Pro-Tek (see Ch. 1)
Help needed: None

Car hoses and tubes are made of steel, rubber, cloth, or even cardboard, but they all carry fluids. The fluid they carry determines which material they are made of. If warm air is all that flows through a hose, it can be made from heavy cardboard or cloth. If hot, but not too hot, liquid—like radiator fluid—flows through them, they can be made of rubber or plastic. If a tube carries very hot gases, it must be made of steel.

The exhaust pipe is a steel tube for carrying hot gas away from the engine. The gas is so hot that it would melt rubber and burn cloth or cardboard. After thousands of miles of driving, the heat and gas actually rust the exhaust pipe from the inside out. Then it must be replaced. This isn't hard, but it may require some more tools than you have. Chapter 18 discusses exhaust system replacement.

Gasoline and brake, power steering, and transmission fluids usually flow through metal tubes or rubber hoses. These fluids must be kept in strong hoses because leaking could cause serious accidents or fires. Since rubber can break, rubber gasoline lines are covered with cloth or steel wire to strengthen them. These hoses hook to other things with special, screw-type clamps, called hydraulic fittings. If the connections or hoses leak, they must be tightened or replaced using special flare nut wrenches. Since these wrenches are expensive and rarely used, let a service station mechanic do this work.

The hoses that carry water and antifreeze from the radiator to the engine and back again are usually rubber. Engine heat slowly cracks the rubber and, after two or more years, they may leak or break. If too much radiator fluid leaks out, the engine can't be properly cooled. It may overheat. Car owners must replace cracked hoses.

There are two large radiator hoses, one at the top of the radiator and one at the bottom. Look at them carefully with a flashlight or troublelight. Press your thumbnail into the rubber to see if it springs back when you take your thumb away. If it doesn't or if there are tiny cracks in the hose, it needs replacing—before it starts to leak. Some car owners replace all radiator hoses every two years when they change antifreeze. Their hoses don't usually leak.

Ali looks at a badly cracked oil vapor hose. She presses her thumbnail into the hose to see that it leaves a lasting mark, but in this case, she can already see the cracks. There are good, noncracked hoses nearby.

Radiator and oil vapor hoses are replaced the same way.

It's a good idea, and fairly cheap if you do it yourself.

Auto parts stores have replacement radiator hoses. Ask for a top or bottom hose (or both) for your make, model, and year of car. You may also need the engine size. All this information is in the car's owner's manual, which you can take to the store with you. Also buy one aviation-type hose clamp for each end of the new hose. Note that different ends of some hoses are different sizes. Get proper sized clamps. These clamps are much better than the ones most car makers use and they are cheap, too.

Some water and antifreeze from the radiator is lost during hose replacement. Therefore, have some extra antifreeze mixture ready. Check Chapter 7 for directions on mixing water and antifreeze and adding them to the radiator.

A screwdriver, pliers, and very sharp knife are needed for hose replacement. If you have no screwdriver, buy an eight- to ten-inch long new one. Its handle should be comfortable in your hand. Try it. Cheap screwdriver tips sometimes break when you turn them hard. The broken piece of steel can fly into your eye. Therefore, it's worth paying a little more for a good screwdriver that won't break. The same companies that make socket wrench sets (Chapter 10) make good screwdrivers. Watch for a sale and get a set of screwdrivers that will last a lifetime.

Before removing hoses, be sure the car is parked, with the engine off, parking brake set, outdoors, on level ground. If the car was driven recently, let it sit for an hour to cool off. Hot water might burn you if you work on the car too soon after it's been driven. Wear old clothes. Be positive the car's owner has given permission to do the work. Pro-Tek can be smeared on your hands now, if you want to use it.

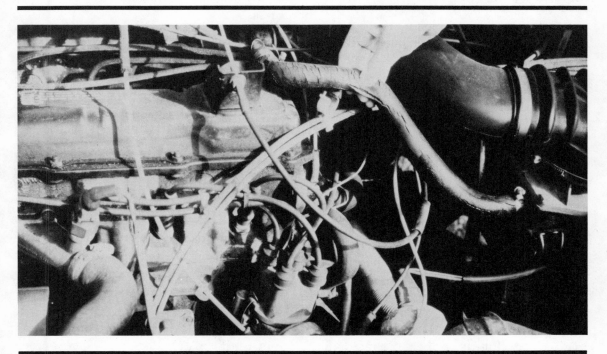

Find the radiator drain wing-nut at the bottom of the radiator. If necessary, ask a gas station mechanic to point it out. You should be able to turn it with your fingers.

Now loosen the old hose clamps. Use a screwdriver for screw clamps or a pliers for pinch clamps. If they're rusty and stuck, break the old clamps. You're going to replace them anyway.

The radiator drain plug is usually opened by hand. If yours needs a wrench, use one. Turn it in the direction shown by the arrow. Joel has just opened the plug. Now he watches the coolant drain out. Be careful of hot radiator fluid.

If only the top hose needs replacing, open the wing-nut and drain a little fluid out until there's no more in the top hose. Take off the radiator cap and look inside. When the fluid level is below the top hose, close the wing-nut with your fingers. If the bottom hose needs changing, open the wing-nut all the way and drain all the fluid. Keep the wing-nut clean and replace it when the radiator is empty. Tighten it with fingers only.

Be sure to catch the radiator fluid in a tub. You may telephone your local pollution control authority or health department to ask them if they have a special place to get rid of old radiator fluid. If they do, take it there. If not, you can get away with pouring the old fluid on the ground and flooding it with lots of water from a hose. Radiator fluid doesn't pollute as badly as old motor oil.

Ali loosens the hose clamps on the cracked hose by turning their screws counterclockwise. They are aviation clamps and are easy to loosen with a screwdriver. Wire pinch-clamps need a pliers and are often rusty. If necessary, break the old clamps and put on new ones.

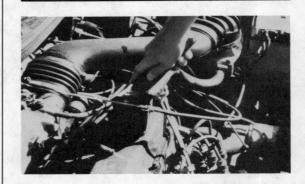

If the old hose sticks on, you may need to cut it off. Ali cuts into the cracked hose with a sharp knife. It may be hard to cut a hose, but don't give up. Since you're replacing it, there's no need to be neat about cutting it.

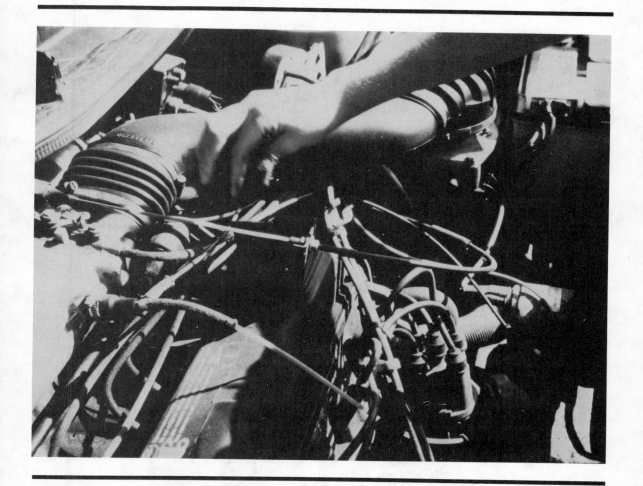

Old hoses often stick to the radiator fitting. If the old hose can't be pulled off, carefully cut it off. Since it's cracked anyway, you don't care about ruining it. Cut only the hose, not yourself. Usually, when one side is completely removed, the other side pulls off. Now relax. That was the hardest part of the job.

The tube where the hose hooks onto the radiator may have rust or bits of rubber sticking to it. Rub them off with a piece of steel wool. When the fitting is clean, wipe any steel wool bits away with a rag.

Place a new clamp loosely around

Fittings where the hose connects to the engine or radiator may be rusty. That may make them leak. Ali rubs the fitting with steel wool to get any rust off. After that, she wipes any steel wool bits away with a rag.

each end of the new hose and push it onto the radiator fittings. If it's hard to push, put some water with antifreeze in it on the inside of the hose. That will make it slippery. Push and twist each end about two inches onto the radiator fitting. This may be hard, but don't give up.

Since Ali's replacing an oil hose, she rubs a few drops of oil on the inside of the new hose to make it easier to put on. Whatever fluid the hose carries can be rubbed on its inside to make replacement easier.

Finally, she puts good clamps on the hose and pushes it on. Tighten the clamps with a screwdriver only enough to make them snug, *not* as tightly as you can turn.

With the new hose in place, position the clamps about one-half to three-quarters of an inch in from each end of the hose. Tighten the clamps with a screwdriver until the steel band *begins* to make marks in the rubber. This won't seem very tight, but it's tight enough. *Never* tighten aviation hose clamps as tightly as you can turn a screwdriver. That can break the hose or cause leaks. Tighten both clamps the same. Now refill the radiator according to the directions in Chapter 7.

Good job! You have saved a lot more than money by doing this one. Consider what happens if the radiator hoses leak badly. The car can overheat and may stop completely. I have been stopped dead in the middle of a busy street during rush hour because my radiator hose broke. It wasn't any fun. But now, that will never happen to you. Take a bow—then wash your hands.

13. WASHING, POLISHING, AND WAXING

Difficulty: Moderate
Parts: Auto polish
Auto wax
Tools: Bucket
Sponges
Laundry soap
Rags
Garden hose and water
Boots
Help needed: None

Wash your car in the morning and it's sure to rain in the afternoon, right? Then, the mud and dirt on the road will cover the nice, clean car. All your work will be ruined.

That's the joke, anyway, but it doesn't work that way. In fact, if you clean the car properly, rain, mud, and road dirt will slide off. After a storm, the car will still look clean if you polish and wax as well as wash. Also, proper cleaning makes the paint last longer and helps prevent rust.

Washing, polishing, and waxing a car is caring for the paint. Rain, mud, snow, sand, and—most of all—salt are enemies of auto paint. Ice-melting salt on winter roads actually attacks paint and steel. It causes rust fast. Therefore, washing off the salt is important. Removing sand and mud helps, too. Where sand scratches the paint,

This car has rust holes and dull, faded paint. Washing, polishing, and waxing won't fix the rust, but they may help slow it down. The water on the paint sticks to it. This is called "sheeting." Polished paint makes water stay together in "beads."

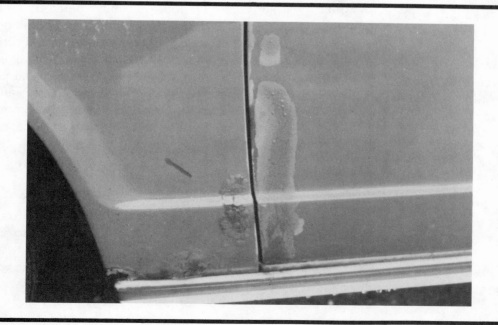

salt and water attack the steel.

The sun ruins paint, too. New cars shine. Notice the dull paint on old cars. It used to be new and shiny, but the sun dulled it. Washing doesn't help old, dull paint, but polishing does. Polishing actually rubs off the "dead" paint. Only shiny paint is left. This is good because bright, shiny paint repels water. Therefore, a good polishing helps to keep water off the steel. That slows down rust.

Waxing is similar. It slows down the sun's dulling and makes water "bead" on the paint. If water forms little beads instead of wetting all the paint, it doesn't cause rust as quickly as nonbeaded water. So, if you want your car to look better and last longer, wash it, polish it, and wax it.

Have the car parked outside, but not in the sun, with the engine off and the parking brake set. Never wax a car in direct sunlight. You need a hose, bucket, sponges, laundry soap, and a nice day. First wash the whole car with warm, soapy water from the bucket. Remove all the sticky dirt. The most important part of washing the car, however, is washing all the cracks and the underbody. Most people can't do a perfect job on the underbody of their car. That is where most of the winter salt eats the steel. Use a hose to spray under the car. Get as much salt and dirt off as possible. Then wash off the soap.

If the car is a few years old, you may notice that the paint is still dull in spite of the washing. It doesn't shine like new. Polishing can bring back the new shine, but it's much harder work than washing. Buy some auto polish at a department, drug, or auto parts store. Many brands work. You need rags, too. Follow the directions on the can and rub the polish onto the paint as hard as you can. Polish a small area at a time. The whole job can take one person several hours. If you get tired, you can do the job in several parts. For example, polish the hood, then rest. Later, polish the fenders, then rest. Still later, do the doors and roof, then rest. You don't need to do the whole job at the same time. Notice that "dead" paint will color your rags as you polish, but the car shines like new. Of course, shiny paint needs no polishing.

Some polishes claim to wax at the same time as they polish. They may be right, but that might not be a good idea. It certainly makes things easier because you don't have to keep working after the hard polishing job. Still, you usually don't need to polish the whole car each time you wax. Therefore, a polish and wax combination may waste a lot of time and effort. Only polish those parts of the car where paint is dull. Wax goes on everywhere, every time.

Wax, unlike polish, coats the paint. Over dull, "dead" paint, it won't make the car shine. Over shiny paint, it helps protect the paint from the sun's dulling it. It also helps keep water, salt, and dirt from attacking the paint. In many waxes, the coating material is silicone. Silicone is very slippery. Water, mud, and salt can't stick to it. In fact, nothing sticks to it. It makes a good protector for the car's body.

Now, if your car is all shiny, buy some auto wax at a department, drug, or auto parts store. Follow the directions on the can and protect the finish. Never wax the car in direct sunlight. Sun can harden wax and make it almost impossible to spread. The job needs to be done every two to six months or so, but be careful not to wax too often. It is easy to wax over old wax. When that happens, the layers of wax begin to look slightly yellow. Yellow, waxy build-up

David washes with soap and water in the cracks as well as in the easy places. Joel gets under the car as much as possible.

David and Joel apply auto polish to the car and rub it as hard as they can.

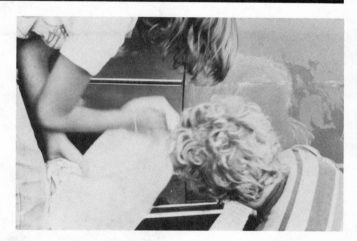

Joel's rag is starting to get pink. He's rubbing old, dead paint off the car. The shiny paint is all that's left after polishing.

The car is in the shade. David rubs wax on. Hard rubbing isn't needed. After the wax dries, he rubs off the dry wax (called "buffing") to let the paint shine.

Now that the paint is washed, polished, and waxed, water doesn't stick to it. It sits in beads that dry rapidly and so won't cause rust as quickly as sheeted water would.

needs to be removed with a special wax remover, a chemical sold in auto parts stores. Avoid having to use it by not waxing too often. Do the job when water won't "bead" on the paint anymore.

After the car has been polished and waxed, keep watch for dull spots in the paint. These may take months to appear, but when they do, you can polish them without polishing the whole car. As long as the car is shiny, you just wash and wax it every few months to keep it looking like new and to help prevent rust. It's not really much work and, if you have kept up with it, you won't ever have to polish the whole car again. The really hard work is already done. Keep after it and it's easy.

14. TIRES

Difficulty: Moderate
Parts: None
Tools: A U.S. penny
Tire pressure gauge
Tire pump or compressor
Hand soap and/or Pro-Tek (see Ch. 1)
Help needed: None

Four hands push and steer cars...well, sort of. The part of each tire touching the road is about as big as your hand. Therefore, rubber the size of four hands steers and pushes.

Since so little rubber touches the road, every bit of it must count. In good weather, it does. Rubber grips a dry road very well. Steering and speeding up are easy.

In bad weather, water, mud, slush, or snow can come between road and tires. Then, no matter how many tires the car has, they can't push or steer it. They push and steer the water, mud, slush, or snow. The wheels spin and the car runs out of control. That causes accidents.

To help prevent accidents, tire makers do three things: (1) design and build tires with as much rubber as possible touching the road, (2) put treads in the tires, and (3) make wider tires. Some tire materials and designs allow more rubber to make contact with the road than others. At least some rubber must touch the road in order for a tire to push or steer a car. The more rubber that does so, the better. Treads, those jagged slots in the tire, give rain or snow somewhere to move, away from the tire so that they can't keep the rubber from touching the road. Finally, in some cases, wider tires may allow more rubber to

Radial (left), bias-belted (middle), and bias-ply (right) tires are made of layers of cloth and cords. The cords are wrapped differently in each tire. The way they're wrapped makes the tires hold the road differently and wear at different speeds.

make contact with the road than do narrow ones. This allows better steering and helps prevent accidents.

As always, the tire maker's solutions have problems. Different tire designs and materials make bad weather driving safer. Better designs also cost more. The cheapest tires are bias-ply tires. Better, more expensive ones are bias-belted. The best and highest priced are radial tires. Each has cords made from cloth, fiberglass, or steel in it. Radials have more rubber touching the road than the others. They also last longer. Bias-belted tires touch the road less than radials but more than bias-ply tires. Finally, radials give better gasoline mileage than the others.

Lasting longer, giving extra mileage, and being safer make radial tires worth more to some car owners. Others can't afford them.

Wide bias-ply tires actually allow more rubber to touch the road than narrow bias-ply tires. Therefore, many people say they "handle" better than narrow bias-ply tires. The way a car holds the road while turning, speeding up, or slowing down is called "handling." Of course, they also cost more than narrow tires. Also, some cars don't have enough room to hold larger tires. A car body may need to be permanently jacked up to receive them. That costs even more. Finally, radial tires hold the road about as well as extra wide bias-ply tires. Therefore, the extra cost and problems of wide tires are not usually worth it. Most car owners buy radials instead.

If all this isn't confusing enough, tire makers also sell different tires for winter and summer. Regular tires are designed for dry or wet roads. They push water out of the way or give it a place to go in the treads when driving in the rain. However, the treads aren't wide or deep enough to let snow get out of the tires' way.

In winter, snow tires' deep, wide treads give snow and slush more room to move away than do regular tire treads. They grip dry roads well, too. Unfortunately, their treads make more noise than regular treads. They also wear out on dry roads faster than standard tires.

Some people change tires in the winter. They use regular tires most of the year. When it starts to snow, they put snow tires on the driving wheels of the car. This is fine as long as the treads last.

As any tire is driven, it leaves tiny bits of rubber behind. You have probably seen a strip of rubber on the road where someone started or stopped too fast. The same thing happens slowly all during a tire's life. When there is too little tread left, the tire is "bald" and must be replaced.

In most states, bald tires are illegal to drive because, on wet roads, they slip and cause accidents. Get the car's owner to replace worn tires. He or she can get a traffic ticket if a policeman sees "baldies" on the wheels.

You can measure the tread depth to test for bald tires. Since the only tool needed is a Lincoln head penny, this is called the penny test. There are more expensive tread depth gauges, but the penny test is good enough for anyone except a professional mechanic.

The car must be parked level, with the brake on. Never check tires with the car parked in the street. Wear old clothes.

Find the top of President Lincoln's head on the penny. Push that part into the tread. If the tread covers the top of Lincoln's hair on the penny, the tire is good. If the tread is too shallow to hide any hair, replace the tire. Check different spots on each tire to be sure. *Any* worn-out tread anywhere on the tire makes it bald and illegal.

Besides the number of miles a car is driven, the amount of air in the tires affects how long they last. Too much or too little air makes the tread wear unevenly. Too much air wears out the center of the tread. Too little air wears out the edges. Either way, the tires' life is shortened.

At left is a "bald" tire. Next to it is a new tire with lots of tread. The bald tire was driven too long and all the tread wore off. Look carefully at the center of the bald tire and you can see a little tread barely showing.

Joel checks a tire with a penny. Lincoln's hair is covered by the outside of the tire when he puts the penny into the tread, which shows the tire is still good.

The tire at left had too little air in it. Its edges are bald. At right is another tire that had too much air in it. Its center is bald. Both tires are illegal to drive, but both would still be good if the right amount of air had been in them. Keeping the right air pressure in your tires makes them last longer.

Ali unscrewed the tire stem cap to check the air pressure in the tire. Unscrew by turning counterclockwise. The four tires on the wheels *and* the spare tire in the trunk must be checked for proper pressure.

Measuring tire air pressure and keeping it correct helps tires last as long as possible. To measure the air pressure, get a tire pressure gauge. They cost about two to four dollars at department or auto parts stores and look like a small, steel stick. There are two kinds. One's mouth is in a straight line with the rest of the gauge. The other's mouth is pointed at an angle. The straight one is a little easier to use. Ask for the "straight-line" or "in-line" gauge.

With the car parked, brake on, unscrew the cap from the tire's stem. Do *not* lose that cap. Hold the gauge's mouth straight over the stem. Be sure it's straight.

Ali checks the air pressure by pushing an air pressure gauge straight onto the air stem. Arrow A shows the direction she pushes. Arrow B points to the place to read the air pressure. The number (next to the gauge's body) on the stick coming out of the gauge is the tire's air pressure.

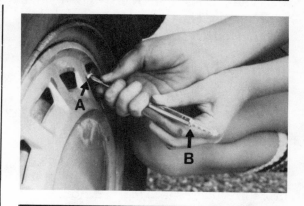

Ali pumps air into the tire with a foot pump. It's slow work, but easier than a hand pump.

Push hard and straight onto the stem. If air escapes around the sides of the gauge, you didn't hold the gauge straight and the reading will be off. Push the sliding stick back into the gauge and try again. Measuring air pressure takes practice. When almost no air (just a *pfft*) escapes, your reading is correct. Read the air pressure on the rear part of the gauge that slides out of the steel stick. The number next to the gauge body is the air pressure in pounds per square inch. Mechanics usually call it "pounds" for short. Replace the air stem cap.

Now check the car's owner's manual for the proper tire pressure. If the pressure on the gauge is within one pound of the number in the manual, good. If it's low, put more air in. Check all tires the same way. Don't forget the spare tire.

Air is added to tires with a tire pump. There are hand or foot air pumps and electric pumps. The hand or foot pumps cost from ten dollars up. They may tire you out, but they use no electricity. You supply the power. Electric air compressors are more expensive, but easier to use. There are small ones that plug into a car's cigarette lighter. They pump tires slowly. Big air compressors at gasoline stations supply lots of air quickly. Of course, if you aren't near a gas station, they aren't very helpful.

If you use a hand pump, read the pump's instructions. Attach its hose to the tire stem. Pump. If you are at a gas station, there may be a handle and air gauge attached to the air hose. Set the gauge for the pressure your owner's manual indicates. If there is no gauge, just use the hose. Press the end of the hose onto the air stem. It's like the air pressure gauge. If you have trouble, ask for help at the station.

After adding air, check the air pressure with the gauge again. If you accident-

ally put too much air in the tires, push the steel or plastic bump on the pressure gauge into the air stem. That will let air out. Then, check again. If you let too much out, refill the tire. Put air in and check. Let air out and check. Only stop when the pressure gauge says you have the right amount of air for that car in those tires. Notice that radial tires sometimes require different air pressure than bias-ply or bias-belted tires.

Except when checking or adding air, be sure to keep the air stem cap on the stem. The cap keeps dirt and mud out of the tire's air valve. Dirt can make the valve leak. Leaky air valves cause flat tires. If yours are leaky, add enough air to get to a gasoline station and ask them to fix it. It takes about five minutes and isn't expensive. To avoid dirty air valves, keep the cap on.

In any case, never, but never ride on tires with much too little or much too much air. Overinflated tires cause poor tread wear and, worse, blow-outs. Blow-outs often cause serious accidents. Badly underinflated tires also cause poor tread wear. Riding on flat tires ruins them and maybe the wheels, too, beyond repair.

She put too much air in, so she must let some out by pressing the little bump on the gauge into the air stem. Some gauges have the bump on the top of the gauge, some on the bottom. The insert shows an in-line and an angled gauge. The arrows point out the bumps for letting out air.

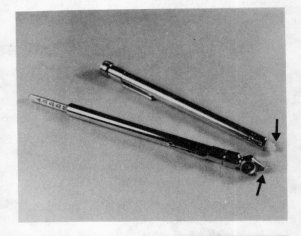

15. CHANGING TIRES

Difficulty: Fairly tough
Parts: Spare tire
Tools: 2 wheel chocks
Jack
Jack handle
Jack base
Lug wrench or socket wrench
Torque wrench (optional)
Screwdriver
Anti-Seize compound (optional)
Penetrating oil
Marker pen or piece of chalk
Rag
Stiff brush
Rubber hammer
Jack stands or cement blocks
(if changing two or more tires)
Hand soap and/or Pro-Tek (see Ch. 1)
Help needed: One adult

Tires don't wait for a rainy day to go flat, it only seems that way. They do wait for a nail, piece of broken glass, other "road hazard," or leak to let their air out. Unfortunately, when your tire is flat, you can't wait. It must be changed *at once*. Most flat tires are repairable if they're changed immediately. Once you drive the car on them, even for fifty feet, they may be ruined.

There's another reason why you might want to change tires. Some auto designs make tires wear unevenly. To prevent this, some drivers "rotate" tires once a year.

"Rotating" the tires helps them last longer. It should be done once a year. If you have bias-ply or bias-belted tires, the diagram at top shows where they should be moved. If you have radial tires, the diagram at right shows their rotation pattern.

Tire Rotation

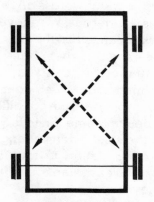

Bias and Bias-belted Tires

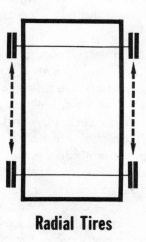

Radial Tires

They take each tire off and put it on a different wheel. If each tire is used in each position, all tend to wear evenly. Some people rotate the spare tire, too. Your tire rotation plan is shown in your car's owner's manual.

Whether changing tires by choice to increase tread life or because of an emergency flat, the watchword is SAFETY. Jacking a car is dangerous. Whenever the car is on a jack, it can fall off the jack. If part of you is under the car when it falls, you may not have that part to call your own anymore. No matter how wet, cold, muddy, bumpy, or unpleasant the conditions, your life and health come first. If you can't change a tire safely, don't change it at all. Pay a service station to tow the car if necessary. Never risk an arm or leg just to save money.

Traffic is another danger for tire changers. Flat tires on a car's left side are especially dangerous. Never change one on the street. Passing cars have hit people as they bend over to pick up a tire. If a left tire goes flat on the street, tell the driver to very s-l-o-w-l-y drive the car completely off the road. If that driving ruins the tire, better it than you.

The car must be completely off the road, parked on a *hard, level* surface with the engine off. Park in a driveway, parking lot or garage where there's no traffic. Set the parking brake *firmly* and wear old clothes. Place stick shift cars in reverse, automatic transmission cars in "park." Since tires are heavy, adult help may be needed. Still, you can do most of the work. Read this whole chapter and have your adult helper read it, too, before beginning work. Pro-Tek hand protector will help you clean up after this job. If you use it, put it on now.

For practice, tire rotation is better than changing a flat. Plan tire rotation for a dry, sunny day and park the car in a safe place.

Some tools are needed. You need three wheel chocks. These may be steel, costing two or three dollars each. They can also be thick, flat rocks or short pieces of thick scrap lumber. Rocks and lumber scraps are free. A jack, jack handle, jack base, and lug wrench come with the car. If only one tire needs to be off the ground at a time, this is all you need. The jack alone is fine for changing one tire. For changing more than one tire at a time, use jack stands. If two or more tires must be off the ground at the same time, use two (or four) jack stands or large cement blocks. For rotating four tires without the spare, you'll have to put the whole car up on jack stands. For most cars, one-and-one-half-ton jack stands work. They cost from three to six dollars each and are sometimes on sale at department stores or auto parts stores. Only use jack stands on a hard, level surface. A car can fall off stands that aren't straight or that slip in soft ground. *Never* use only three jack stands: that leaves the fourth tire hanging in the air, which is dangerous.

Also, jack stands are adjustible. Always use the lowest possible setting that will hold the tires barely off the ground. I rarely use the steel pin that raises the jack stand. If possible, leave it out completely. If you need to use it, it must go all the way through its holes on *both* sides of the jack stand.

If you have some cement blocks around, you can use them to hold the car up. Lay them on their sides, as if you're building a wall. Do *not* place them on end or put weight on the parts that hold the sides of the block together. That could be dangerous.

Place wheel chocks under the two wheels at the other end of the car from where you place the jack. For example, if you are jacking a front tire, place wheel chocks behind the rear wheels. If you jack the rear tires, the chocks go in front of the front tires. Place the third chock on the other side of one already chocked tire.

Carefully read the instructions in your car's owner's manual for the car jack. There are many kinds and each is differ-

ent. Some attach to the bumper and some under the side of the car. Be sure you understand the directions before using the jack. Take it out of the trunk and put it in place, but *do not* jack the car yet.

For changing a flat tire or rotating the spare tire, remove the spare from its storage space. Make sure the spare or replacement tire has enough air in it. Look at Chapter 14 about checking tire air pressure. If you can't lift the new tire, ask your adult helper to get it out for you. Place it next to the tire you plan to remove. Don't jack the car yet.

Ali puts a "chock" (a rock, the other one is steel) behind one of the wheels.

Slip a large screwdriver tip or the end of the lug wrench under the edge of the tire's hub cap or wheel cover. Pry the cover off. Place it on the ground near the tire, but out of the way.

Now comes the hardest part of the job: loosen the lug nuts. The screws sticking out of the wheel are called lugs. The nuts on them are lug nuts and the wrench for turning them is a lug wrench. Place the lug wrench on one of the lug nuts. Push hard counter-clockwise in short jerks. Sometimes, jumping on the handle helps. If the nut loosens, great. Sometimes, lug nuts are so tight that you can't loosen them. If this happens, some penetrating oil may help. Ask at an auto parts or department store for penetrating oil. There are many brands and all work. Get the nonspray can. Sprays cost too much for the small amount of oil you get. Place a few drops of penetrating oil on the lug threads at the base of the nut. Wait a few minutes for it to work. Try again. If you still can't loosen the lug nuts, ask for help. Loosen the lug nuts of each wheel *just before* jacking it. When

Ali pries the hub cap off with a screwdriver. The hub cap protects the lug nuts from road dirt and makes the wheel look a little better. It's easy to remove.

With the car still on the ground, wheels chocked, Ali loosens the lug nuts with a lug wrench. The nuts are very tight. She can't loosen them using just her hands on the wrench, so she pushes the handle of the wrench down with her foot. It's always easier to push down than to pull the wrench handle.

all the nuts on the wheel are loose, stop. Do not remove them, yet.

Ask your adult helper to check the jack. It must be straight under the car. If everything is all right with him or her, you can jack up the car.

someone at a service station. Watch as a mechanic puts your car on the lift. The places the lift touches the auto frame are good for jack stands, too. Never just put jack stands or cement blocks anywhere. Some parts of a car's underbody are deli-

With the lug nuts loose, Ali positions the jack straight up under the side of the car as the jack directions say. The arrows shows that the jack is straight. She jacks the car up so that the wheel no longer touches the ground.

Never put any part of your body under part of the car that could fall. Only jack the car high enough to raise the tire off the ground. If you need to use jack stands, jack the car high enough to get them under the frame, no higher. Extra jacking wastes effort.

Removing two or more tires at the same time requires two or more jack stands, one for each tire you want to take off. The best way to know where to place the jack stands or cement blocks is to ask

cate. They cannot hold the whole car's weight. After positioning a jack stand or cement block, carefully lower the car onto it with the jack. Make sure it stands straight, not at an angle. If it's crooked, jack the car back up. Straighten the stand or block. Lower the car again. Remove the jack and, if you're replacing more than one tire, repeat this process with the next wheel.

If you're rotating tires and have no spare to rotate, always place either the front or back of the car on stands before jacking the other end. That is, place the front on stands before jacking the rear; place the rear on stands before jacking the front. *Never* try to place diagonal wheels on stands alone. Car frames are not designed to take that kind of stress. Also, don't forget the wheel chocks.

Joel wants to rotate the tires so he positions jack stands at strong places under the car's frame. Such places (arrow) are often strengthened with extra steel.

Look at the loose lug nuts. Sometimes the front of the nut is the same as the back. Sometimes not. If your lug nuts are different on the side that goes toward the car from the side that faces out, mark them with a felt-tipped pen or piece of chalk. Remember how to put them back on. Then, with the wheel off the ground, completely remove the lug nuts. If the threads are dirty, you may need to use the wrench. Place each nut into the hub cap or wheel cover. Don't lose any.

After the lug nuts are off, imagine the wheel as a clock face. Place your right hand between the four and five (about 4:30) and your left hand between the

Joel holds two lug nuts in his hand. One side is flat. The other is tapered. If yours look like this, replace them with the tapered side pointing *toward* the car.

Ali finally takes the tire off the lugs. The 12, 3, 6, and 9 of a clock face on the tire make her hand position clear. She holds the tire at about 4:30 and 7:30 on the tire's imaginary clock. Don't lose the lug nuts.

seven and eight (about 7:30). Never put any part of you under the six! Lift slightly and remove the wheel. Be sure not to drag the wheel across the lug threads. It might damage them. If the tire is too heavy, ask for help. Put the tire out of the way.

Carefully clean dirty or rusty lugs and lug nuts with a rag or stiff brush. If you want them to be much easier to remove next time, buy a small can of Anti-Seize Compound at an auto parts store. Anti-Seize costs about five dollars for a small can, but it will probably last for the rest of your life. Inside the lid is a brush. Wipe most of the silvery goo off the brush back into the can. Anti-Seize Compound is powerful. A little goes a long way. Carefully paint a very thin layer of goo on the lugs. Don't use too much. This prevents rust and makes nut removal easier next time.

To make nut removal easier next time, she paints a little Anti-Seize Compound on the lugs before putting the new tire on.

Turn the replacement tire on edge so that the outside faces you. The outside is the part that holds a hub cap. Also, the inside usually has a deeper space for mounting than the outside. With the outside of the wheel facing you on the ground, place your hands at 4:30 and 7:30 again. Lift (or have your adult helper lift) the tire and put it on the lugs. Each lug hole in the wheel must have a lug coming through it. Don't let the wheel damage the lug threads. Partially screw on each lug nut. Be careful that nuts that are supposed to face in, do.

If you were changing or rotating several tires, you used jack stands or cement blocks to hold the car up and now must position the jack to jack the car again. Only jack high enough to release the jack stand. Remove it. Lower the car enough for the tire to firmly touch the ground. Tighten the lug nuts firmly with the lug wrench. Lower the car all the way and remove the jack. This process must be repeated for every tire that was held up on a stand.

Remember the torque wrench for tightening spark plugs in Chapter 10?

After putting the new tire on, Ali tightens the lug nuts by hand as much as she can. Then she lowers the car. With the car on the ground, she uses the torque wrench for final tightening. The torque wrench's pointer indicates 55 foot-pounds.

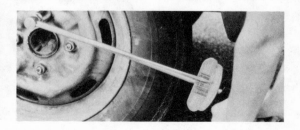

Reread that chapter. Torque wrenches measure force exerted in a circle. If you can afford one or already have one, use it. Find a socket that fits the lug nuts and put it on the torque wrench. With the car on the ground, held still by the wheel chocks, tighten each lug nut to fifty-five (55) foot-pounds. If all are tightened to the same torque, one is much less likely to loosen or fall off. All will hold the wheel in place firmly and will be easier to remove the next time you need to change tires.

If you don't have a torque wrench or the right-sized socket, tighten the lug nuts with the lug wrench. Tighten *almost* as hard as you can. Try to tighten the same amount on each nut. The Anti-Seize Compound will help nut removal next time.

Unless you are going to change all four tires, now's the time to put the jack away and remove the wheel chocks. Replace the hub caps or wheel covers by fitting them over the wheels and pounding them on with your hands or a rubber hammer. Never use a steel hammer to replace hub caps. Position the cover so that the tire's air stem sticks out.

If you just replaced a flat tire, take the flat to a service station. They may be able to fix the hole or leak with a plug. Repaired,

plugged tires are just as good as they were before the puncture. Plugging a flat is much cheaper than buying a new tire.

After practicing changing tires in a safe place, think about doing it in bad weather or in the mud. In mud, you need something wide and hard to put the jack on. Otherwise it'll sink into the mud instead of raising the car. In bad weather, you may get soaked or half frozen. In any case, anyone who drives a car should be able to change tires. You must be able to handle an emergency so that you don't become one.

By the way, if you used the Anti-Seize Compound and the torque wrench for this job, you did it as well as the best professional mechanic. Your care will show the next time you change tires. It'll be a snap then.

With all the lug nuts tightened to the same torque, Ali replaces the hub cap. She positions it so that the air stem sticks out through its slot in the hub cap (arrow). Then, she hits it on each side, firmly, with a rubber hammer. Never use a steel hammer; it'll damage the hub cap.

16. LUBRICATING THE FRONT END

Difficulty: Fairly tough
Parts: Grease
Tools: Grease gun
Rubber or plastic extension
Jack
Jack handle
Jack base
Jack stands or cement blocks
Wheel chocks
Rag
Flashlight or troublelight
Hand soap and/or Pro-Tek (see Ch. 1)
Help needed: One adult

Do you like bumpy roads? Imagine how the car's joints feel about them. As wheels bounce over bumps and holes, the steering linkages and auto frame must remain attached. Therefore, the connections between steering wheel, tires, and frame must flex. Since steel doesn't bend well, ball joints are built next to each front wheel. The joints where the steering links with the wheels, springs, shock absorbers, and frame are called the "front end." The joints, like your shoulders, turn in all directions. Of course, as they turn, steel rubs against steel. That causes friction, heat, and wear. If friction isn't reduced, the joints wear and get loose and wobbly.

To reduce friction, lubricate. For the ball joints, thick grease is used. Each joint has a box around it to keep dirt out and grease in. This case has one or more bumps, called grease nipples, where grease goes in. When all the space around the ball joint is packed with grease, the joint is as slippery as possible.

During rain or snow storms, water hits the box. Some grease is washed out. After a while, there isn't enough grease to lubricate the joint and more must be added. If this isn't done often enough, the ball joints wear and become loose. Adding more grease is called lubricating the front end.

Like changing oil (Chapter 4), lubing takes place every few thousand miles. Check the sticker on the side of the driver's door for the odometer reading when the car was last lubricated. If there is no sticker, ask the car's owner when the job was last done. Subtract the sticker number from the present odometer reading. The remainder is the number of miles the car has gone since its last lubrication. Check the owner's manual for how often the front end should be lubed. If the car has been driven the right number of miles, it needs lubricating. How about doing it yourself? You can do it as well as a gas station mechanic and save money, too.

The tools needed are a jack, jack handle, jack base (all come with the car), wheel chocks, two jack stands or cement blocks, a grease gun, a grease cartridge, some old rags, and a troublelight or flashlight. If you changed tires in Chapter 15, you know how to use the jack and, perhaps, jack stands. Grease guns are sold in auto parts and department stores along with grease cartridges to go inside them. They cost about eight to ten dollars and the cartridges cost about one dollar. Try to buy a gun with a rubber or plastic extension between the body and grease fitting. If you can, spend extra money for a separate rubber connector. It makes the job much easier. Each grease cartridge does several lube jobs. The cost of the grease gun is made up in the money saved in the first one or two lubes.

An adult helper should check to make sure the jack and jack stands are properly in place, help load the grease gun, and press its fitting onto the grease nipple. That sometimes requires a lot of strength. Ask your adult friend to read this chapter and Chapter 15 before beginning. Also, be sure you have the car owner's permission to do the lube job.

The car must be parked on a level surface (*not* the road) with the engine *off* and parking brake *on*. Put the transmission in reverse (for stick shift cars) or in "park" for automatic transmission cars. Wear old clothes. This is a messy job so you can make clean-up easier by putting Pro-Tek on your hands now.

Read the directions and load the grease gun. If you have trouble, ask for help at an auto parts store. Your adult helper may be able to help, too. This is sometimes a job for a strong person.

Read the jacking instructions in the owner's manual and Chapter 15 again. Jacking a car can be done safely, but if you can't do it properly, don't do it at all. Remove the jack, jack handle, and base from their holders. Before jacking, be sure to chock the rear wheels with rocks or pieces of lumber. Position the jack carefully. It must be straight. Jack up one side of the car. Position a jack stand or cement block under a strong part of the car frame. Ask a service station mechanic where your car's frame is strongest. Don't place the stand just anywhere. It could damage the car's underbody. Make sure the stand is straight. If possible, use the stand in its lowest position with the steel pin completely out. If you must raise the jack stand, the steel pin must go through the holes on *both* sides of the stand. If you use cement blocks, they must be on their sides, *not* on end. Use them as if you were building a wall. After one side is done, do the other. The whole front of the car should be off the ground and on stands now.

One more warning: never crawl under a car that's held up only by a jack. Jacks are wobbly and dangerous. They can fall. Jacks only lift cars, they don't hold them up. Use jack stands or cement blocks and take no short cuts.

Now the hard part: finding the grease nipples. Crawl under the front of the car with a troublelight or flashlight. Near the wheels are lots of rods and pipes. Look for little bumps on the ends of these. They're probably covered with oil, grease, and dirt. Wipe them clean with a rag. One or more may be nuts, but at least one on each side usually has a tiny hole in the center. That's it! Clean it carefully. Find *all* the nipples on both sides and, sometimes, in the center. Wipe them clean. If you can't find any, ask a garage mechanic to point them out. Also note: there's at least one car today that has no grease nipples at all. Some Subarus have none and there may be other cars without grease nipples. Look carefully before you buy all the tools needed for lubricating the front end.

The grease nipple at the top is covered with dirt. In the middle, Noelle wipes the nipple clean with a rag. The clean grease nipple at bottom is ready for the grease gun. Any dirt on the nipple may be pumped into the ball joint.

Make sure the grease gun's grease fitting is completely clean. Any dirt on the fitting or nipple will be pumped into the ball joint and make it wear. Careful cleaning makes the difference between a fast, sloppy job and a slightly longer, first-rate job. Don't skimp on time.

Press the grease fitting onto the grease nipple. You'll feel a soft snap or jerk as the fitting is pressed into place. A flexible extension on the grease gun makes snapping the fitting on the nipple easier. After the fitting snaps into place, it'll hold onto the nipple by itself.

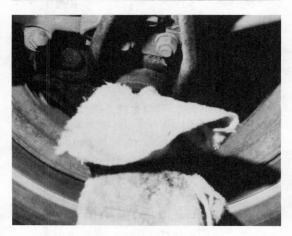

Noelle pushes the grease gun's fitting onto the grease nipple. She pushes hard.

To the right, a grease cartridge is shown. Its end caps are removed before putting it into the grease gun. Unscrew the gun's cap or, with some guns, the head. Put the cartridge into the gun and replace the gun's cap. You're ready to go. There are other ways to get grease into a grease gun, but this is the quickest and easiest.

Try to work the pump handle. If grease comes out the sides of the grease fitting, it wasn't snapped on properly. Push harder and get it to snap. If you can't, ask for help.

Slowly pump the grease gun handle. Make sure to pull the handle all the way up and press it all the way down. The gun pumps grease at about eight to ten thousand pounds of pressure per square inch. When grease begins to leak out of the ball joint case or the rubber above the joint swells up, stop. Pull the grease fitting off the nipple. If there are more grease nipples, do each the same way. Grease both the right and left sides of the car. There are no grease nipples in the back because there are no ball joints there. Still, some older cars need their universal joints in the rear greased, too. Check for grease nipples in back and grease any you find. Then, you're done.

Jack up the car slightly, remove the jack stand, and lower the car all the way. Do the same on the other side. Remove the

Finally, Noelle pumps grease into the ball joint by moving the grease gun's handle up and down. Arrow A points to the grease gun. Arrow B points to its rubber extension, which makes pushing the fitting onto the nipple easier. If grease leaks out the sides of the gun's fitting, it isn't snapped on the nipple tightly. Try again. When the rubber "boot" above the nipple swells and starts to leak grease, you're done.

wheel chocks. Make sure there's no dirt on the grease gun fitting and put the gun away where it'll stay clean. Write down the odometer reading. It lets you figure out when to lube the car again.

Congratulations. You just saved from five to ten dollars. Of course, the grease gun costs that, but the next time the car's owner will make money. Maybe the owner will share the savings with you. Before you ask about that, wash!

17. VALVE COVER GASKET

Difficulty: Long, dirty, and tiring
Parts: New valve cover gasket
Tube or can of gasket cement
Tube of liquid thread-lock
(like Locktite Lock 'n' Seal)
Tools: Socket wrench set
Screwdriver
Open end, box end,
or combination wrenches
Torque wrench (optional)
Carburetor cleaner (spray can)
One gallon of kerosene
Tub
Butter knife or putty knife
Wire brush
Steel wool
Garden hose and water
Rags
Rubber gloves
Old newspapers
Masking tape
Marking pen
Plastic cup
Small paint brush
Hand soap and/or Pro-Tek (see Ch. 1)
Help needed: One adult

When you look at your car's engine, is it covered with oil and dirt? It shouldn't be. If there's oil everywhere, something is leaking. Oil leaks waste expensive oil. They also make the engine compartment and the garage floor a mess. This makes auto work dirtier than necessary. Besides, an oil leak can foul your air filter. Why not fix it?

Unfortunately, finding the leak may be hard. If the filth is very thick, some people have a service station clean their engine with steam. That is expensive, but some-times worthwhile. If the leak is from the side of the engine's top cover, you're in luck. That's the valve cover. You can remove and replace the leaky gasket yourself.

The valve cover gasket leaks at arrow A. Arrow B points to one of the bolts holding the cover on. Most covers have six or more bolts.

A gasket is a rubber, plastic, cork, metal, or even paper ring that seals the gap between two touching metal parts. Since gaskets aren't as strong as the metal around them, they can leak in time.

An engine's valves let gasoline and air into the cylinders at the proper time for burning. To do this, they move up and down. That movement involves rubbing and that means lubrication to make the steel slippery. Oil pumped over the valve stems helps them move smoothly. The valve cover and its gasket seal the oil in the engine so it isn't lost.

The valve cover gasket may wear out or a service station may sometimes install it incorrectly after valve adjustment. Before buying parts, make sure the valve cover gasket is your problem. Auto engines have valves directly over (or beside) their

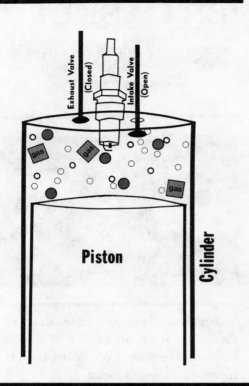

Each auto cylinder has two valves next to the spark plugs. One lets gasoline and air in, the other lets burned gases out. The intake valve shown here lets gas and air in. This prepares for a spark.

Since each cylinder has two valves and all valves must have covers, if you know where the cylinders are, you can always find the valve covers. In most cars, cylinders are in a line, or half are on one side and half on the other side of the engine. The second way is called a "V" engine. Cylinders for an in-line or "slant 6" engine are on the left. Some cars only have four cylinders in a line. The V engine's cylinders are at right. Some cars have six cylinders or four cylinders arranged in a V.

Cylinder Arrangement

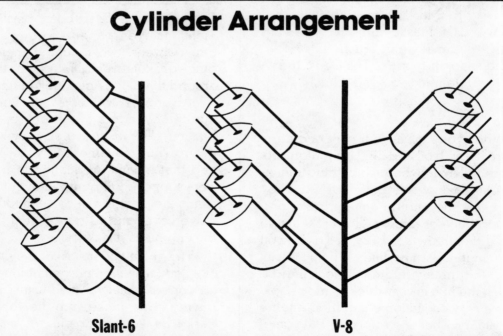

Slant-6   V-8

cylinders. Cylinders are located in a straight line down the middle of the engine or in a V on either side. If yours is a V-4, V-6, or V-8 engine, two, three, or four cylinders are on either side of the engine. If you have an in-line four or six cylinder car, the cylinders are in the middle. In the slant-six engine, they slant toward one side. The valve cover sits directly over the cylinders. It's either on top, in the middle of the engine, or, in V engines, there are two covers, slanted to each side, like a V. Either V engine cover could leak. Look for fresh oil with little or no dirt in it where the cover meets the rest of the engine. As the oil spreads out, it catches dirt and is hard to tell from very old oil.

You can remove the valve cover and replace the gasket as well as any service station. However, there's a catch. This is a long, dirty job. It can take a few hours. Once you start, you must finish. The car can't run without the valve cover in place. Still, if you do it properly, your engine should stay clean for years.

Before deciding to replace the valve cover gasket, read this whole chapter. Figure out what you need to do before starting. Make sure the whole procedure is in your mind. Check with an adult who can watch or check each step before you continue.

Once you decide the valve cover gasket is bad and you really want to see this job through, buy one part: a new gasket. For V-4, V-6, or V-8 engines, buy two. Get a gasket for your make, model, and year of car at an auto parts store. The engine size may be needed, too. Take your owner's manual for this information. New valve cover gaskets cost about four or five dollars. They are delicate. Handle them with clean hands and great care. If you

tear the cork or rubber in a new one, the store won't take it back. You'll have to buy another.

You also need tools and fluids. A socket wrench set, a screwdriver, perhaps some small open-end wrenches, a torque wrench, a small tube or can of gasket cement, a tube of liquid thread-lock (like Lock 'n' Seal), a spray can of carburetor cleaner, one gallon of kerosene, an old tub, an old butter knife or putty knife, some steel wool, a wire brush, a working garden hose, rags, rubber gloves, old newspapers, masking tape, a felt-tipped pen, a plastic cup, and a small, old paint brush are needed. If you bought a socket set for changing spark plugs (Chapter 10), a screwdriver for changing hoses (Chapter 12), and some open end wrenches for removing battery cables (Chapter 9), use them. If not, reread those chapters and buy or borrow the tools. Get gasket cement, liquid thread-lock, carburetor cleaner, and kerosene at an auto parts store. The cement, thread-lock, and carb cleaner cost from one to three dollars for a little tube of the first two or a spray can of the third. Kerosene costs about $1.50 per gallon if you supply your own gallon container. The tub, steel wool, wire brush, and rags are for cleaning. Rubber gloves protect your hands from the kerosene. It can sting. You may want to use Pro-Tek for still more protection. If so, rub it on your hands now.

The torque wrench is special. You can use the one purchased for installing spark plugs and tires, but it's really too big. A three-eighths-inch drive torque wrench looks like a little brother to the bigger one. It's made for tightening small hexagonal (six-sided) headed bolts. If you tighten one of the valve cover bolts too much, the new gasket will leak. With the torque wrench, you know exactly how much force to use on each bolt. Some mechanics depend on their experience to know how much to tighten bolts. Beginners should use a torque wrench. If you can't afford a small beam-type torque wrench, some auto parts stores rent them for a dollar or two per day. If you can't afford the torque wrench, this job can be done without it, too. Use an ordinary socket wrench and try to tighten all screws or bolts the same amount. But it's much better to have the torque wrench.

Some valve covers are held on with slotted screws. Check yours. If you have slotted screws, there are torque wrench adaptors for them. The stores that sell torque wrenches also sell adaptors. Phillips-head screws need no torque wrench.

Have the car parked on a level surface with the engine off and the parking brake on. If possible, do this job outdoors, but *not* in the street. If the engine has been running for a while, let it coool before starting work. Hot engines burn hands. Wear old clothes. This is a very messy job.

Many things may be in the way of removing the valve cover. Only move the things you must. The spark plug wires might be in the way. If so, carefully mark each with a piece of masking tape. Number each wire and each plug with a marker pen on the tape so you'll know which wire goes to which plug. *The order matters!* Wire number one should go to plug number one and so on. After they're all numbered, pull each wire off of its plug and move it aside.

The air filter housing (reread Chapter 2) may be in the way. If so, remove the air filter and its housing. Some housings are held to the engine. If yours is, find the screws or bolts holding it. Carefully re-

The air filter housing is in the way of removing the valve cover so Ali must take it off. She loosens the one bolt that holds the air filter housing to the engine. She uses a small socket wrench with the right sized socket.

move them with a socket or open end wrench. Place the housing, filter, screws, and everything attached aside. Put a *clean* rag over the top of the carburetor to protect it. Don't drop anything, even the smallest bit of dirt, into the carburetor. Also, don't lose any of the pieces you have removed. Mark them with masking tape and a marker. You'll have to replace them properly when you finish.

If any hose is in the way, try to bend it out of the way. Only unhook what must be unhooked. Some hoses break upon removal. You must replace them. Some hoses may be attached to the valve cover with clamps. Unscrew only the clamps to free the cover. Again, don't remove a hose unless you must.

Once everything is out of the way, remove all the screws or bolts holding the valve cover. Since these bolts are probably covered with oil and dirt, place them in an old plastic cup with enough kerosene to cover them. If there are washers around each bolt, put them in the cup, too. Don't lose anything. The kerosene softens and removes most of the oil and dirt.

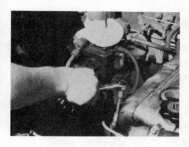

She then removes each bolt that holds the valve cover on. All the bolts are placed into a cup of kerosene. None are lost. The clean rag covering the carburetor's top keeps dirt out.

Slowly lift the valve cover. If it comes up, good. If not, engine heat has stuck the cover and gasket to the engine. In that case, carefully push a butter knife or a putty knife into the gasket. Slowly work your way around the valve cover, loosening the gasket. Don't try to completely free the cover at only one spot. That might bend it. Once it's bent, it's ruined and must be replaced. Since new valve covers are

Since the valve cover is stuck, Ali pushes a putty knife into the old gasket and slowly moves it around the valve cover. The arrows show that she moves it in and out and, at the same time, around the cover.

expensive, be careful not to ruin the one you have. If the valve cover and gasket are stuck to the engine, this removal process may be long and hard. It took me four hours on one car. Don't rush; keep at it. You will succeed. Put the cover aside in a tub of kerosene.

With the cover off, you're looking at the tops of the valves and part of the mechanism that oils and lifts them. Keep it clean. If bits of gasket stick to the engine, clean them off with a wire brush. The two surfaces where the valve cover meets the engine must be clean. If they aren't, the new gasket may leak. Now wash your hands and put on the rubber gloves.

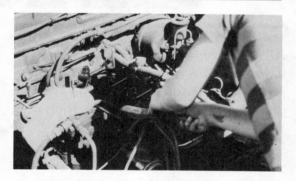

After the valve cover is off, Joel cleans bits of old gasket from the engine with a wire brush. Don't use steel wool here. Steel wool bits may get into the engine and damage it.

Position the valve cover and tub where splashed kerosene doesn't matter. Clean both the cover's inside and outside with rags and steel wool until they gleam. This is a big job, but it's important. Make sure all the old gasket is removed and thrown away. The gasket surface must be clean or the new gasket will leak. Keep at it. All the work pays off soon. Wash the old oil and dirt away with kerosene.

Ali cleans the valve cover in a tub of kerosene. She wears rubber gloves to protect her hands. She uses steel wool on the cover and will also use it on the bolts in the cup when the cover is finished.

Clean the bolts or screws in a cup of kerosene. Use a rag, steel wool, and then soap and water. Rinse everything in clean water. Any dirt, oil, kerosene or soap left will prevent the bolts from holding tightly. All screws and washers must be clean and dry.

When the valve cover is as clean as possible, take it out of the kerosene and place it on the lawn, driveway, or parking lot. Wash it with a strong blast from the garden hose. If you missed a spot, go back to the kerosene. Wash with water again. Make sure every nook and cranny is clean and steel wool bits are gone. Dry the cover with a rag. Put it aside.

After cleaning the valve cover with steel wool, there are tiny steel wool bits all over it. Ali gets rid of them by spraying the valve cover with water. Use a strong spray and hit every part of the cover. When all the steel wool is gone, dry the cover with a rag.

By now, everything should be clean except for the screw holes in the engine. Spray carburetor cleaner into them one by one. Don't get any in your eyes or mouth. It's poisonous and burns eyes, but it cleans well. If the holes are very dirty,

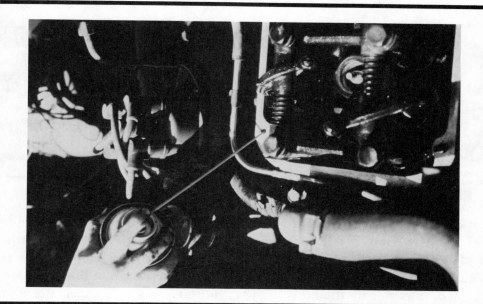

Before replacing the gasket, she cleans the bolt holes by spraying carburetor cleaner into them. Most spray cans have a plastic extension with them that makes spraying right into the holes easy. Keep the cleaner away from your eyes and mouth.

twist a rag or tissue and push it into each hole to get the dirt out. The thread-locking liquid won't work in a dirty screw hole. When all the holes are clean, let them dry for five minutes. Wash the rubber gloves and remove them. Wash your hands again. If you are using it, put another coat of Pro-Tek on your hands.

Prepare for sticking the gasket and valve cover together with gasket cement. Spread out old newspapers where there's no wind. Fit the new gasket on the valve cover. Take it off and turn it over onto the newspapers. Spread a *thin*, even coat of gasket cement on one side of it. Keep the other side where it touches the engine

Ali spread some old newspaper and placed the new gasket and clean valve cover on it. She spread a thin coat of gasket cement on the new gasket and has already put some on the cover. The cement comes in small cans or in tubes. If you buy a tube, you must supply your own brush. The cans usually have brushes inside their covers.

clean and cement-free. Use a small, old paint brush to even out the cement. Spread another thin coat of gasket cement on the part of the valve cover that will touch the gasket. Let it partially dry, keeping all dirt

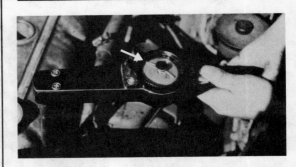

After letting the gasket cement get tacky on both the cover and gasket, Ali carefully joins them. Her hands are clean and she gets no dirt, dust, or grit on any surface that is joined by the cement. Also, she lines up the bolt holes in the cover with those in the gasket. If any cement gets on the wrong side of the gasket, carefully clean it off with a rag and some kerosene.

away. Now carefully join the cemented side of the gasket and the valve cover. Make sure the bolt holes in the cover and gasket line up. Press the two together.

Now everything goes back together. Carefully place the valve cover and gasket on the engine. All the bolt holes must line up. Screw each bolt in with your fingers. When they are all finger-tight, use a screwdriver if they have driver slots or a socket wrench if they have hexagonal heads. Go slowly. Tighten each bolt with the screwdriver firmly, but *not* as tightly as you can. If you're using the socket wrench, when the tightening begins to firm up, switch to the torque wrench. Torque each bolt to five (5) foot-pounds. Do this in a pattern beginning at the right middle bolt, then the left middle bolt. Then do the bolt next to the first one. Now move to the bolt

After replacing the valve cover and putting all the bolts on by hand, Ali tightens them with a 3/8" torque wrench. This is a dial torque wrench and is smaller than the one used to tighten the spark plugs and wheel lug nuts. The arrow indicates that the wrench's pointer says 5 foot-pounds. Three-eighths inch torque wrenches are sold as beam-type wrenches, too. Beam torque wrenches are much cheaper than dial wrenches. Some of them, however, only read in inch-pounds. Five foot-pounds equals sixty (60) inch-pounds.

Looking down on the valve cover, the bolts are numbered in the order in which to tighten them.

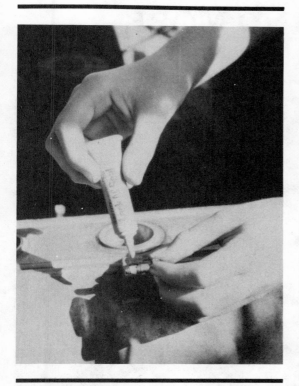

After torquing all the bolts, Ali removes the first one and puts a drop of Lock 'n' Seal, a screw-locking chemical, on it. She then replaces and torques the bolt with the Lock 'n' Seal on it to 5 foot-pounds. She does the same (in the same order) to all the bolts.

across from that, and so on. When all the bolts are torqued or screwdriver tightened, stop.

Now the touch that will make your work last years: use Locktite Lock 'n' Seal or one of the other thread-locking chemicals on the market. Remove the bolt from the middle of the right side of the cover. Shake the tube of thread-locking liquid. Place *one drop* on the bolt's threads. Replace it in the hole and tighten it to five foot-pounds again. Don't touch that bolt again. Remove the one across from it, shake the thread-lock, put on one drop, and torque that one to five foot-pounds. Continue putting thread-lock on each bolt in turn and torquing them until all are done. The thread-lock holds the bolts in place with the proper tightness. None can loosen from the car's shaking as it drives down the road. Proper torque, thread-

locking liquid, and careful cleaning are the most important steps.

Replace hoses, clamps, air filter housing and filter, spark plug wires (in the correct order), or anything else you had to remove to get the valve cover off. If screws are oily, clean them in the kerosene, just as you did the valve cover's bolts. You can use the liquid thread-lock for any screws that you want to stay put while the car shakes its way down the road. Be sure the screw and screw hole are clean or the thread-lock won't work. When you must remove the screw next time, thread-lock will release it. It only protects against vibration loosening a screw.

Pour the dirty kerosene back into its can for later use. If it's so dirty that you don't want to reuse it, pour it into your used motor oil bottle or jug (Chapter 4). Clean all tools so they don't rust. Put them away where they can be found for later jobs. Also, return any tools you borrowed cleaner than when you got them. If you rented a torque wrench, return it clean and in good condition. If you return it dirty, you may be charged for cleaning it. Finally, cap the gasket cement and thread-lock tightly. Store the gasket cement on he shelf. Thread-locking compound lasts longer if stored in a refrigerator.

If you do everything as well as you just replaced that valve cover gasket, you can be a pro at anything you like. I salute you.

You have done some ambitious work, but there's always more. You added antifreeze and water to the radiator. You can also change all the coolant and clean the radiator. Old, cracked spark plug wires are changeable at home. Telling what's wrong with the engine by looking at the spark plugs is possible. Brake, transmission, and power steering fluids are replaceable at home. You can even replace the whole exhaust system. In fact, you can learn to do almost anything the car needs with experience, a few books, and the right tools. You already have some experience and tools. Now for the books and a few suggestions.

The Clymer's Publication Company (12860 Muscatine Street, Arleta, California 91331) and the Chilton Book Company (Chilton Way, Radnor, Pennsylvania 10989) publish repair manuals for every car made today. Their books cover everything from changing the oil to overhauling the engine. They are in bookstores and auto parts stores for eight to twelve dollars. Though they have pictures and explanations, most aren't as detailed as this book's. Both companies expect you to know what parts and tools to buy and how to use them. If, for example, your valve cover gasket leaks, Clymer's *Repair Handbook* and Chilton's *Auto Handbook* (or most of the other car care books they publish), say nothing about it. They think you should know how to repair a bad gasket. After reading Chapter 17 of this book, you do.

The exhaust system, which includes the exhaust pipe, muffler, and tail pipe, is a good example of what Clymer's and Chilton's do and do not explain. If there's something special about your car's exhaust system, the repair books explain it. If the pipe just bolts to the manifold over a gasket and bolts to the muffler and tail pipe, all they say is what the beginning of this sentence says. You must know that some parts have to be replaced and others may be reused. Usually, the U-bolts that hold everything up are very rusty. They must be replaced. If the exhaust pipe is still good, but the muffler is rusted through, only replace the muffler.

Another thing Clymer's and Chilton's rarely explain is the best tool for doing a job. The socket wrenches and open-end wrenches should remove almost all bolts or nuts. Sometimes, nuts and bolts are rusted in place. Penetrating oil often helps, but few books say anything about it. Socket wrench extensions, universal joints, and breaker bars are available. Read about them in tool catalogs. Anti-Seize Compound helps once the bolt is off, but you must know about it. In other words, most books depend on your knowledge and experience to fill in the details of what to do. Use your head and you'll be fine.

If you plan to work on many different cars, Chilton's *Auto Handbook* is popular and Chilton's *Easy Car Care Book* has

good information in it. The *Auto Handbook* costs about seventeen dollars and the *Easy Car Care Book* costs about ten. Be sure to buy the foreign car handbook if your car wasn't made in the United States. Both books tell about many different cars. Neither has as much detail as the repair handbook for your specific car. If you don't want to buy these books, there are always libraries.

Both Clymer's and Chilton's discuss spark plug deposits. They have pictures of what the spark gap looks like when gasoline is burning properly and when something is wrong. If, for example, there's oil leaking into the cylinders, the plugs will have a black, gummy material on them. The pictures in these books help to recognize the exact problem. Once you know what's wrong, read the chapter in the book on that problem. Then you can decide to repair it yourself or take the car to a mechanic. Whichever you choose, you now know if the mechanic knows what he or she is doing. You have knowledge and that puts *you* in control.

There are also many books from other publishers on auto care. *Popular Mechanics Magazine* publishes *Basic Car Care Illustrated* which has many good pictures that help find parts you might have trouble with. *The Big Book of Auto Repair* (published by Petersen's) has useful information. So does Arco Publishing, Inc.'s *The Weekend Mechanic's Handbook: Complete Auto Repairs You Can Make*. Goodheart and Willcox have written *Automotive Encyclopedia* and so on and so on.

It might surprise you to learn that the automobiles listing in *Books in Print*, a book that lists all books published today, covers about eighteen small print pages. There are hundreds of books. They talk about every part of a car. For example, there are nineteen books about car prices. There are twenty books on Toyotas. Books have been written about every car on the road from the Avanti to the Willys. There are books on brakes, electrical systems, fuel systems, lubricating, classic cars, racing cars, auto history, how cars work, painting cars, and even model cars.

Some books are for very little children. *My Little Book of Cars and Trucks* is for children from kindergarten to third grade.

Other books are for older kids. *What Makes a Car Go?* by Scott Corbett (Little, Brown and Co., 34 Beacon Street, Boston, Massachusetts 02106) and *Compacts, Subs, and Minis: Be Your Own Mechanic* by David J. Abodaher (Julian Messner, 1230 Avenue of the Americas, New York, New York 10020) are interesting. For someone considering a career as an auto mechanic, read *Here Is Your Career: Auto Mechanic* by C. William Harrison (G.P. Putnam's Sons, 200 Madison Avenue, New York, New York 10016).

The point is that there are books on any subject you're interested in. All you have to do is go to your local library. If they don't have a book, ask them if they can get it for you. If you want to change the brake fluid and don't know how, there are always books on your car that have pictures and have explanations.

Another source of information is auto parts and tools manufacturers. DuPont and Prestone, for example, explain how to change radiator fluid on jugs of antifreeze. Prestone makes a special tool for "back flushing" the radiator. That's a special, and very easy, kind of cleaning. The kit costs about three dollars. You can install it yourself. Both companies make cans of fluid for cleaning rust out of the radiator. They explain themselves on the can. Many other tools and devices are described and explained by their makers. Always read directions. You can write letters to manufacturers asking questions. All of them want to sell their products and will be glad to tell you things you might not have known. They figure you're more likely to buy their products if you know how to use them than if you don't.

Also, you can ask questions at auto parts stores. Often, the person behind the counter knows a lot about cars. He or she wants to sell parts and tools. Therefore, that person may be happy to explain them to you, hoping that you will buy them. If, for example, you have problems with the spark plugs after putting in new ones, the wires may be bad. Do they have tiny cracks in them? Look carefully. If so, go to an auto parts store and buy a new set of spark plug wires for your make, model, and year of car. Ask the person behind the counter to tell you how to replace them. If the store isn't too busy, he or she can probably explain it very well. Of course, if the store is very crowded, the clerk has no time to help. So try to go to an auto parts store to ask for help when it's not busy. Saturdays are usually very busy. If possible, try to go on a weekday morning.

So you see, if you need to fix something on a car or you can't figure out what's wrong, there's always a book or person with the answer. Keep searching and asking. The only time you won't get help is after you give up. Try the library (librarians are very helpful), the bookstore, the local gas station and auto parts stores, even parts manufacturers. Write letters. Ask questions. There are no secrets, only questions you haven't yet asked. Keep at it.

INDEX